book 2

Composition Practice

THIRD EDITION

A Text for English Language Learners

Linda Lonon Blanton

University of New Orleans
New Orleans, Louisiana

HEINLE
CENGAGE Learning™

Australia • Brazil • Japan • Korea • Mexico • Singapore • Spain • United Kingdom • United States

PF

Composition Practice, Book 2, Third Edition
Linda Lonon Blanton

Vice President, Editorial Director ESL/EFL: Nancy Leonhardt

Acquistions Editor: Sherrise Roehr

Managing Editor: James W. Brown

Sr. Production Editor: Maryellen Killeen

Marketing Manager: Charlotte Sturdy

Sr.Manufacturing Coordinator: Mary Beth Hennebury

Composition: A Plus Publishing Services

Project Management: Anita Raducanu

Photo Research: Lisa LaFortune

Illustration: Len Shalansky

Cover Design: Gina Petti, Rotunda Design

Text Design: Julia Gecha

For product information and technology assistance, contact us at **Cengage Learning Customer & Sales Support, 1-800-354-9706**

For permission to use material from this text or product, submit all requests online at **cengage.com/permissions** Further permissions questions can be emailed to **permissionrequest@cengage.com**

ISBN 13: 978-0-8384-1998-4
ISBN 10: 0-8384-1998-4

Heinle
20 Channel Center St.
Boston, MA 02210
USA

Cengage Learning is a leading provider of customized learning solutions with office locations around the globe, including Singapore, the United Kingdom, Australia, Mexico, Brazil, and Japan. Locate your local office at: **international.cengage.com/region**

Cengage Learning products are represented in Canada by Nelson Education, Ltd.

Visit Heinle online at **elt.heinle.com**

Visit our corporate website at **www.cengage.com**

Printed in United States
12 13 14 15 16 17 14 13 12 11 10

Preface

This third edition of *Composition Practice, Book 2,* celebrates the continuing successful use of the series by many thousands of English learners. This edition should prove helpful for students who need practice in the kinds of writing found on state standardized tests. The basic instructional design and pedagogy remain the same, but several new features have been incorporated in response to user suggestions.

A pre-reading activity has been included in each unit, and post-reading caption-writing exercises are integrated with the all-new illustrations. A list of new vocabulary is also now included in each unit along with a master vocabulary list in the appendix and a list of irregular verb forms. An optional open-ended activity, *Connecting,* encourages students to develop computer skills by searching the Internet for information related to unit themes. Additionally, the grammar progression is slightly accelerated in that it now includes the past continuous contrasted with the simple past. An index allows teachers to locate skills found in state standards and on tests.

Book 2 is divided into ten units. Each unit contains an illustrated reading passage, followed by exercises on comprehension, grammar, vocabulary, semantic organization, and/or writing mechanics. An illustrated model composition—which makes use of the vocabulary, grammar, and organization of the reading passage—follows the exercises. Students are then presented with detailed instructions for writing their own compositions. All reading passages and models focus on certain purposes for writing, such as narrating and describing, and certain means of organizing ideas, such as chronological and spatial ordering. The assumptions here are that even on an elementary level there is more to composing than mere sentence-level exercises and that English learners can understand and use sophisticated principles and techniques of English composition writing without waiting until they are more fully fluent in English.

I wish to acknowledge my former colleagues of the English Language Institute at Central YMCA Community College in Chicago. With them I began the work that led to the *Composition Practice* series. Although the school no longer exists, it was an exciting place and time to teach and learn. I would like to give special thanks to my dear friend Linda Hillman, who had faith early on that a textbook or two could emerge from my jumble of mimeographed lessons.

I would also like to thank the reviewers, many of whose helpful suggestions were incorporated into this third edition:

Carol Antunano, *English Center,* Miami, FL

Nancy Boyer, *Golden West College,* Huntington Beach, CA

Miguel A. Contreras, *English Language Institute at El Paso* and *El Paso Community College,* El Paso, TX

Jeff DiUglio, *Boston University,* Boston, MA

Terry Paglia, *Newtown High School,* Elmhurst, NY

Kathleen Yearick, *Groves-Wilmington High School,* Wilmington, DE

Contents

UNIT 1 • Describing Daily Routines   1

Composition Focus: Narration
Organizational Focus: Chronological Order
Grammatical Focus: Simple Present Tense, Frequency Words,
    e.g., *usually, always,* Present Continuous Tense

UNIT 2 • Describing a Friend   13

Composition Focus: Using Description
Organizational Focus: Classification
Grammatical Focus: Predicate Adjectives, Future with *be going to*
    and *will*

To the Teacher

It is commonly said that students learn to read and write by reading and writing. While the adage *is* true, its simplicity belies a complex process of development. This process is complicated enough in a reader-writer's first language and all the more challenging in another language. *Composition Practice* is based on many years of experience in mentoring English learners through this learning process, in large part by creating for them an awareness of rhetorical possibilities, and by providing clear direction, guiding their practice, and giving positive and useful feedback.

● **Who can use *Book 2*?** It is designed for adult students of English on an upper elementary level of proficiency, including those who have already successfully completed *Book 1*. It is intended for people who are learning English for professional, academic, and business reasons. The lessons were successfully tested with students ranging in ages from 15 to 55, who—in total—spoke nine different languages and had educational backgrounds ranging from ninth grade to university degrees. Altogether the lessons provide about 50 class hours of instruction (roughly an intensive 8-to-10-week course).

● **How is *Book 2* organized?** It is divided into ten units, each containing a reading passage, follow-up exercises, a composition to model, and instructions for students' own writing. The readings progress in grammatical complexity in this order: simple present contrasted with present continuous, the *going to* future, simple future *will*, simple past contrasted with past continuous, and present perfect. Many grammar books present English structure in this order, and students will probably be studying grammar and working on reading-writing simultaneously. The model composition in each unit makes use of the same grammar, vocabulary, and organization as does the reading passage.

● **What is the textual focus?** All of the reading passages and model compositions in *Book 2* focus on people like any of us who work, play, study, and live their lives. This is a way to make the content realistic. Collectively, the texts tell the story of a fictional Italian family, the Baronis. Places in New Orleans are commonly mentioned, and most are real, but knowledge of the locale is not necessary for comprehension. Your students will substitute their own neighborhoods and familiar places in their writing.

● **What writing assignments do I give?** Explicit instructions for student writing appear at the end of each unit. You and your students will need to go over the instructions together. In some cases, they may require your interpretation and explanation. After all, you will know what your students can handle and what will confuse them. As students start their writing, closely supervise and you will see if they understand what to do by the way they are following through.

● **How do I use the picture sequence in each unit?** The visuals in each unit should be used for oral practice and writing. You will probably want students to follow the pictures while you read the corresponding text. Then students can narrate the story according to the pictures. Students can also connect words to pictures by writing captions underneath or in their notebooks.

● **What rhetorical rationale governs *Book 2*?** The readings and writing models in *Book 2* are descriptive in purpose (Units 2, 4, 9), narrative (Units 1, 5, 7), and expository (Units 8 and 10). Units 3 and 6 are in letter form: Unit 3, a friendly letter and Unit 6, a business letter. Students can become consciously aware of many fairly commonplace features of English writing as they progress through the materials in *Book 2*. With your students, you will want to look at the diagrams in each unit as visual representations of useful organizational concepts.

● **How much time will the lessons take?** Each unit is designed to provide material for five hours of class work. If your students meet for composition five days a week, all the work can be done in class. If they meet less often, the exercises can be done as homework, and you can still complete a unit a week.

● **How do I pace the materials?** The following is a five-day suggested breakdown of each unit:

DAY 1: Reading
Introduce the context of the reading by involving students in the pre-reading activity, *Before You Read*. Some pre-reading activities lend themselves to group discussion; others to pair or group work. Move then to the actual reading passage, but have students listen first, with their books, closed, as you "tell" the reading once or twice. Next have the students follow silently, this time with their books open, as you slowly read the text aloud. At this point, explain new words and grammar that you think will pose stumbling blocks. Now, have students read silently again—this time on their own, but with dictionaries in hand. There may be words they want to check on. Once they seem satisfied with their reading, ask questions that can be answered directly from the reading. It's fine if students actually find a sentence or phrase that contains the answer to a question and read it aloud. To allow further processing of new words and phrases, write sequential questions on the board and give students a chance to take turns answering without reading from the text. Finally, turn to the sequential pictures and have students write captions for each

one. This aids memory and helps them connect meaning and image. At this point, with the pictures as memory prompts, some students may be able to (re) tell the complete story to the class.

DAY 2: Review and exercises

Use the pictures to refresh everyone's memory of the story. Then, with the story as content for further language-learning work, have students complete the exercises. If possible, have students work in pairs or small groups. If there is enough time, check students' answers orally.

DAY 3: Presenting the model for writing

If the exercises weren't checked earlier, check them now. However, be sure to have the model for writing be the day's focus. Present the model by following some or all of the steps used in presenting the reading text on Day 1. After you and the students work through the model, go over the instructions for students' (next day) writing. Work with students to help them start planning their writing a day ahead, so their ideas can "percolate" overnight. Making an outline may help; you may need to show them how to do this. Make sure, however, that students understand that outlining is a way to trigger thinking and start planning, not a rigid commitment. As they think, especially when they start writing the next day, new ideas may surface.

DAY 4: Writing

Have students write their compositions in class. It's fine if they use outlines, notes, or even check the model periodically to "borrow" a word or phrase. Encourage them, however, not to simply copy. They will want to make their compositions their own, with as much of their own content as possible.

DAY 5: Wrapping up the unit

Finish up any work left over from Days 1–4. If you have read over student compositions, talk about common problems or needs. A mini-lesson on grammar or organization may be in order. In whatever manner you give feedback or attend to common needs, always avoid putting anyone on the spot, except, of course, to hold up a student's work as a positive example. Based on your feedback, students may need to redraft, correct, or expand their writing. If they have access to computers, you'll want to "close" out a lesson with the computer activity *Connecting* at the end of each unit.

● **How do I pace the materials if I have less class time?** If your composition class meets fewer than five days a week, you may take as long as two weeks to complete a unit and still cover most of the material in *Book 2*. The schedule might then work like this:

DAY 1/WEEK 1: Reading

Present the content of the reading according to the steps outlined for Day 1 of the five-day plan (above). Students' homework for Day 2 is to do the exercises.

DAY 2/WEEK 1: Presenting the model for writing

Check homework in class by having students take turns giving their answers. Do this as quickly as possible in order to focus on the model and on preparing students for their own writing by going over the instructions in the unit. In presenting the model, follow some or all of the steps followed in presenting the reading on Day 1. Students' homework assignment is planning their compositions in outline or note form, according to your instructions.

DAY 1/WEEK 2: Writing

Go over the model again to review, and quickly check on students' outlines or notes by having them briefly explain their plans. Remind students that their plans may change as they write, and that they should be open to new ideas that may emerge. Students write their compositions in class as you circulate and offer assistance where needed.

DAY 2/WEEK 2: Wrapping up the Unit

Follow the procedure outlined in Day 5 of the five-day plan.

● **What is of ultimate importance if I can't do it all?** No matter what your schedule is, or even the limitations of your teaching situation, have your students do their writing in class, where you can serve as a resource. Help that you provide *while* they are writing is almost always more useful for their writing development than feedback on their papers *after* they've finished writing. When you do provide line-by-line feedback, try to do it in the context of individual teacher-student conferences. A student then has a chance to ask questions, clarify your feedback, and feel more secure about correction.

● **What are the ultimate goals for Book 2?** By the time students finish Unit 10, they should be able to write a short (one-to-two-page) descriptive, narrative, or expository essay on a familiar, everyday subject. A competent reader of the essay should be able to perceive an introduction to the topic, the development of related and relevant content, and a conclusion. The content of the essay should flow in a way that makes sense to a competent reader of English.

To the Student

You will need the following materials:

1. a loose-leaf notebook
2. 8 1/2 x 11 inch loose-leaf notebook paper
3. a pen and pencil
4. a good translation dictionary and a simplified English-English dictionary

You should follow these rules for good reading:

1. Look at the complete reading selection before you use your dictionary.
2. Let your eyes catch groups of words; do not stop after every word.
3. Do not move your mouth when you read; read with your eyes.
4. After you read the complete selection, use your dictionary to find the words you do not know.
5. Read the selection again; look for important connections: and, because, after, before, while, etc.

You should follow these rules for good writing:

1. Leave margins.
2. Indent each paragraph.
3. Put a period at the end of each sentence; put a question mark at the end of each question.

   Example: John is absent today.
   Is he sick?
4. Use capital letters correctly:

   a. names of people

   Example: Peter Andres

   b. names of cities

   Example: Paris

   c. names of countries

   Example: Japan

   d. names of rivers

   Example: the Amazon River

e. names of streets

   Example: Michigan Avenue

f. names of buildings

   Example: the Empire State Building

g. names of organizations

   Example: the United Nations

h. names of national, ethnic, and racial groups

   Example: French, Jewish, African Americans

i. titles

   Example: Dr. Santini

j. the first person singular pronoun: I

k. days of the week

   Example: Thursday

l. months of the year

   Example: April

m. holidays

   Example: New Year's Day

n. titles of books, magazines, newspapers

   Example: the New York Times

o. the first letter at the beginning of each sentence and question

   Example: Are you happy?

Placement of Parts of a Composition

Your Name
Course

Title of your composition

[ ] xxxxxxxxxxxxxxxxxxxxxxxxxxxxxxxxxxx
xxxxxxxxxxxxxxxxxxxxxxxxxxxxxxxxxxxxxxxxxxx.
xxxxxxxxxxxxxxxxxxxxxxxxxxxxxxxxxxxxx
xxxxxxx.
    [ ] xxxxxxxxxxxxxxxxxxxxxxxxxxxxxxxx.
xxxxxxxxxxxxxxxxxxxxxxxxxxxxxxxxxxxxxxx.
xxxxxxxxxxxxxxxxxxxxxxxxxxxxxxxxxxxxxxxx.
xxxxxxxxxxxxxxxxxxxxxxxxxxxxxxxxxxxxxxxxxx
xxxx xxxxxxxxxxxx. xxxxxxxxxxxxxxxxxxxxxx
xxxxxxxxxxxx. xxxxxxxxxxxxxxxxxxxxxxxxxx
xxxxxxxxxxxxxxxxxxxxxxxxxxxxx.
    [ ] xxxxxxxxxxxxxxxxxxxxxxxxxx. xxxxxxxx
xxxxxxxxxxxxxxxxxxxxxxxxxxxxxxxxxxxxxxx.
xxxxxxxxxxxxxxxxxxxxxxxxxxxx.

[ ] indentation

left margin   right margin

Describing Daily Routines

- **Composition Focus: Narration**

- **Organizational Focus: Chronological Order**

- **Grammatical Focus: Simple Present Tense**
  Frequency Words, e.g., *usually, always*
  Present Continuous Tense

1. _____

2. _____

3. _____

4. _____

5. _____

6. _____

7. _____

8. _____

9. _____

10. _____

11. _____

Reading 1

Before You Read

Think about this. Then talk about it with a partner.

What do you do every day? When do you *get up? Eat breakfast? Go to school? Work? Eat dinner? Study?* What are you thinking about or doing right now?

Read

Bruno's Daily Activities

Bruno Baroni lives in an apartment in New Orleans with his mother, father, and older brother. The apartment is small, and he shares a bedroom with his brother. Bruno is a student. He goes to school every day, and he works part time in a music store after school.

Bruno usually gets up about 6:00 every morning. An alarm clock wakes him up. He tries to stay in shape, so he always exercises for ten or fifteen minutes. Then he showers and shaves. He always gets dressed before he eats breakfast. For breakfast, he usually has coffee, toast, and fruit. He doesn't like to eat a big breakfast. After breakfast, he cleans up the kitchen while his brother gets ready for school. Bruno listens to the morning news on the radio while he does the dishes. By 7:30, he and his brother are ready to leave for school. They go to school by car.

Bruno and his brother, Roberto, usually arrive at school at 7:45. Roberto goes straight to class. Bruno goes to the library for about half an hour. Then, he meets his girlfriend, Maria, for a cup of coffee before class. His first class starts at 9:00. He is in class from 9:00 to 12:00. He has three classes in a row. He studies English composition, algebra, and chemistry. Bruno works hard, but he likes his classes. After class, he has lunch with Roberto and Roberto's girlfriend, Sylvia. Then, Bruno gets a ride with Roberto to his job at the music store. Bruno works there three afternoons a week.

Right now, it is 6:30 and Bruno is listening to music and playing his drums while Roberto is talking to a friend on the phone. They aren't studying now. They usually study after dinner. Their father is reading a magazine, and their mother is preparing dinner. Sometimes,

Bruno cooks. He is a good cook. After dinner, Roberto helps with the dishes. Then, Bruno and Roberto study together at the kitchen table. They always have a lot of homework.

All in all, Bruno's days are long and tiring. He enjoys the weekend when he plays his music. During the week, he works hard and he sometimes gets discouraged. Most of the time, however, he feels good about his life.

After You Read

Caption Writing: Please write a sentence under each picture on page 2 or in your notebook.

Vocabulary from Reading 1

Find the words below in Reading 1. Examine the use of each word and see if you can guess the meaning. If you are not sure, ask a classmate or check your dictionary.

Nouns	Verbs	Adjectives
alarm clock	exercise	discouraged
algebra	shave	long
apartment	shower	small
bedroom	wake	tiring
chemistry		
dishes	**Adverbs**	**Expressions**
kitchen table	part time	all in all
magazine	straight	in a row
news	together	stay in shape
radio	usually	

Exercise A: Comprehension/Vocabulary

Please circle the letter below each sentence to complete the sentence correctly. The information comes from Reading 1.

1. Bruno lives in _____.

    a. a house   **b.** an apartment   **c.** a dormitory

2. He lives with _____.

    a. his family   **b.** a roommate   **c.** his cousin

3. He is _____.

    a. a student   **b.** a bus driver   **c.** a carpenter

4. He does exercises because _____.

    a. he is very fat   **b.** he wants to stay in shape   **c.** he likes to play baseball

5. He gets dressed _____.

    a. before breakfast   **b.** during breakfast   **c.** after breakfast

6. He goes to school _____.

    a. by bus   **b.** on foot   **c.** by car

7. After school, he works _____.

    a. at a sporting goods store   **b.** at a grocery store   **c.** at a music store

8. He eats dinner _____.

    a. with his family   **b.** with a friend   **c.** alone

9. In the evening, Bruno _____.

    a. watches TV   **b.** goes dancing   **c.** studies

10. All in all, Bruno's days are _____.

    a. full of fun   **b.** long and tiring   **c.** relaxing

Exercise B: Simple Present Tense (Third Person Singular)

Please list at least ten of Bruno's daily activities. Use the *simple present tense*. Pay attention to the third person singular verb form.

> *Example:*   *Bruno gets up at 6:00.*
> *He does exercises.*

1. _____
2. _____
3. _____
4. _____
5. _____
6. _____
7. _____
8. _____
9. _____
10. _____

Exercise C: Frequency Words

Please rewrite the following sentences. Use the frequency word in parentheses. Be careful with the word order.

> *Example:*   Bruno exercises after he gets up. (always)
> *Bruno always exercises after he gets up.*

1. For breakfast, he has coffee and toast. (usually)

   _____

2. He leaves for school at 7:30. (sometimes)

   _____

3. He goes to school by car. (always)

   _____

4. He is on time. (always)

   _____

5. He goes to the library before class. (usually)

   _____

6. He cooks dinner. (sometimes)

_____

7. Bruno and Roberto watch TV, listen to the radio, or read. (rarely)

_____

8. Bruno goes to bed early. (rarely)

_____

9. He stays up late. (usually)

_____

10. Bruno has a busy day. (usually)

_____

Exercise D: Present Continuous Tense

Please change the statements about Bruno's usual day to tell what he is doing right now. Use the present continuous tense. Change the underlined frequency expression to *right now*.

> *Example:*   Bruno gets up <u>at 6:00 every morning</u>.
> *Bruno is getting up right now.*

1. Bruno <u>usually</u> eats breakfast in the kitchen.

_____

2. Bruno listens to the radio <u>in the morning</u>.

_____

3. Roberto and Bruno drive to school <u>every day</u>.

_____

4. Bruno <u>often</u> has coffee with Maria in the cafeteria.

_____

5. Bruno and Roberto <u>sometimes</u> work <u>in the afternoon</u>.

_____

6. <u>On the weekends,</u> Bruno plays the drums with his friends.

_____

7. Bruno <u>sometimes</u> cooks dinner for his family.

_____

8. Roberto and Bruno <u>often</u> listen to music in their bedroom.

_____

Exercise E: Simple Present Tense vs. Present Continuous Tense

Please write the correct form (simple present tense or present continuous tense) of the verb in parentheses.

> *Example:* Bruno **_is doing_** exercises right now. (do)
> He usually **_works_** at the music store in the afternoons. (work)

1. The alarm clock _____ at 6:00 every morning. (ring)

2. Right now, Mrs. Baroni _____ breakfast. (fix)

3. Roberto and Bruno usually _____ for school at 7:30. (leave)

4. Now Roberto _____ to class and Bruno

   _____ to the library. (go)

5. After class, Bruno often _____ lunch with his brother. (have)

6. Roberto always _____ Bruno to work. (drive)

7. Mr. Baroni _____ a magazine at this moment. (read)

8. Bruno _____ to some music now. (listen)

9. After dinner, Roberto usually _____ with the dishes. (help)

10. Roberto and Bruno _____ in the kitchen now. (study)

Notes and Questions on the Organization of Reading 1

Part A: Paragraphs

Reading 1 has five paragraphs. They tell the story of Bruno's daily life and what he is doing at this time. Go back to Reading 1. Be sure that you see five paragraphs. The following questions will help you understand the system of paragraphs in Reading 1.

1. Where do you find information about the beginning of Bruno's day? Which paragraph?

2. Where do you find information about Bruno's school? Which paragraph?

3. Where do you find information about Bruno's evening?

4. What information does the first paragraph give? Why is it there?

5. Look at the last paragraph. It is very short. What does *all in all* mean? Why is the last paragraph there?

Part B: Order

The word "order" refers to what is first, what is second, what is third, etc., in a composition. There should be a reason for what is first, what is second, etc. The following questions will help you understand the order of Reading 1.

1. How much time does the second paragraph cover?

2. How much time does the third paragraph cover?

3. How much time does the fourth paragraph cover?

4. Is 6:00 A.M. before or after 7:30 A.M.?

5. Is 9:00 A.M. before or after 12:00 noon?

6. Is the order in the second, third, and fourth paragraphs from early to late or from late to early?

Time order is called "chronological" order. It can go from late to early or from early to late. Think of different composition topics that might follow time order.

Notice these connecting words in Reading 1:

before	*by* (specific time)
after	*from* (time) *to* (time)
while	*then*

All of these words have a time meaning. Ask your teacher for more examples if you don't understand. Next, go on to Model 1.

1. _____

2. _____

3. _____

4. _____

SCHEDULE
9:00 – 10:00 / CLASS
10:00 – 10:10 / BREAK
10:10 – 11:30 / CLASS
11:30 – 12:00 / LUNCH
12:00 – 1:00 / CLASS

5. _____

6. _____

7. _____

8. _____

9. _____

Model 1 (Narration)

Maria's Day

Maria lives in a small apartment in New Orleans. It is on the second floor of an old building. She lives with her cousin. Maria is a student at Lake College. She is studying psychology. She works part time as a clerk in a department store.

Maria gets up early every morning. She usually takes a shower and gets dressed before she has breakfast. She doesn't usually have much time for breakfast, so she has only a piece of toast and a cup of coffee. After breakfast, she quickly cleans up the kitchen. Then, she leaves for school. She always goes to school by bus.

Maria arrives at school about 8:30. First, she goes to the cafeteria to meet her boyfriend, Bruno, and have another quick cup of coffee. Then she goes to class. She is in class from 9:00 to 1:00. She has a ten-minute break at 10:00 and a half-hour break at 11:30. She has lunch during her long break. After class, Maria goes to work. She works at Maison Blanche, a busy department store downtown. She works in the hat department. She likes her work and she likes to talk to the customers. She works very hard. At 5:00, she finishes work. Then, she takes the bus back home. It takes her half an hour to get home.

Now it is evening, and Maria is having dinner. Her cousin is working late, so Maria is eating alone. She is listening to the radio while she is eating. After dinner, she always does the dishes. Then, she studies. She usually goes to bed late because she has a lot of homework.

All in all, Maria is a very busy person. She works hard and studies hard. She misses her family in Mexico, but she has a good life.

Caption Writing

Please write a sentence under each picture on page 10 or in your notebook.

Composition 1

Instructions for Student's Composition

1. On 8½ x 11 inch loose-leaf notebook paper, write a composition about your daily activities and what you are doing or thinking right now. Give your composition a title.

2. Write five paragraphs. Remember to indent and leave margins. Put the following information in your paragraphs:

   PARAGRAPH 1.   Introduce yourself. Where do you live? What do you do?
   PARAGRAPH 2.   Tell about what you are doing right now. Where are you writing? Are you using a computer or paper and pen? Where are you sitting?
   PARAGRAPH 3.   Tell about your morning activities (before work or school) and about the main part of your day.
   PARAGRAPH 4.   Tell about your evening activities.
   PARAGRAPH 5.   Conclude with several general points.

3. Take what you need from Model 1. Let it help you with grammar, vocabulary, and ideas.

4. Your composition should look like this:

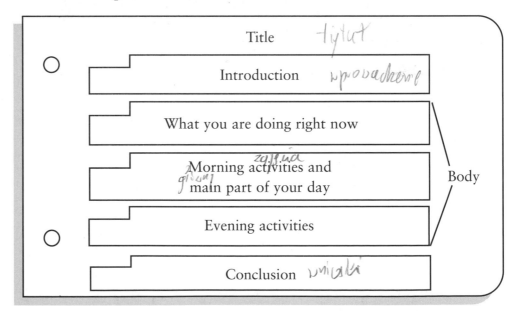

 # Connecting

Use a search engine (such as Netscape, Yahoo, or Excite). Think of a music group or song that you like. Can you find information about it? Tell a partner about it.

Describing a Friend

- **Composition Focus: Using Description**

- **Organizational Focus: Classification**

- **Grammatical Focus: Predicate Adjectives**
  Future with *be going to* and *will*

1. _____

2. _____

3. _____

4. _____

5. _____

6. _____

7. _____

8. _____

9. _____

Reading 2

Before You Read

Think about this. Then talk about it with a partner.

Do you have a good friend? Is your friend tall or short? What does your friend look like?
What about your friend's *personality*? Is your friend serious? Pleasant? Kind? Fun?

Read

My Friend, Roberto

Roberto is one of my good friends. He is also my brother! We go to school together and we play soccer together. We live together. We even share a bedroom. Of course, we also share our parents! I think that we are going to be friends for a long time. We will certainly be brothers for a long time!

Roberto is 21 years old. He is about 5 feet, 9 inches tall. His face is long and narrow. His eyes are green. His hair is dark brown. He doesn't look very Italian. He smiles a lot and usually has a friendly look on his face. He isn't fat and he isn't thin. His build is average. He plays soccer and baseball, so he stays in shape. He doesn't like to dress up. He likes to wear jeans and T-shirts.

Roberto has a pleasant personality. He is fairly outgoing, but he is also very sensitive. He worries about our parents because they work so hard. He also worries about our grandparents because they are old. Our grandfather is also ill. Roberto often writes to both of them. He is my older brother, but my English is better than his. He is a little sensitive about that, too! Roberto is crazy about strawberry ice cream and soccer.

Roberto's future plans are not very definite. First, he is going to improve his English. Then, he is going to study science and physical education. He wants to be a high school coach. After that, I don't know what he will do. He has a girlfriend and he likes her very much. Is he going to marry her? I don't know, but I hope so. I want him to be happy. He is a good person and a true friend.

After You Read

Caption Writing: Please write a sentence from the reading under each picture on page 14 or in your notebook.

Vocabulary from Reading 2

Find the words below in Reading 2. Examine the use of each word and see if you can guess the meaning. If you are not sure, ask a classmate or check your dictionary.

Nouns	Verbs	Adjectives
build	dress up	average
coach	improve	dark
future plans	marry	definite
jeans	smile	fat
look	worry	friendly
personality		green
physical education	**Adverbs**	ill
science	certainly	narrow
T-shirt	fairly	old
		outgoing
	Expression	pleasant
	be crazy about	sensitive
		tall
		thin
		true

Exercise A: Vocabulary

Please find the *antonym* (the word with the opposite meaning). Write it below.

together	*ill*	*future*	*outgoing*	*narrow*
unfriendly	*short*	*thin*	*uncertain*	

1. tall   short
2. shy   outgoing
3. well   _____
4. definite   uncertain
5. friendly   unfriendly

6. past   future
7. wide   narrow
8. alone   together
9. fat   thin

Exercise B: *Be*/Predicate Adjectives

Please rewrite the following sentences. Use *is* or *are*. Put the adjective after the verb and put the noun before the verb. Use *His* at the beginning of each sentence.

Example: He has a long face.
His face is long.

1. He has a narrow face.

    His face is narrow

2. He has green eyes.

    His eyes are green

3. He has dark hair.

    His hair is dark

4. He has brown hair.

    His

5. He has a friendly look.

    His look is a friendly

6. He has a pleasant smile.

    His smile is a pleasant

7. He has a pleasant personality.

8. He has an average build.

9. He has interesting ideas.

10. He has indefinite plans.

Exercise C: *Be going to*

Please think of a friend and complete the following. Write full sentences. Use **He is going to** or **She is going to** at the beginning of each sentence. The time is future. You are writing about your friend's future plans, not about Roberto's.

Example: return to his (her) country
    He is going to return to his country. OR
    He is not going to return to his country.

1. become an engineer

 _____

2. improve his (her) English

 _____

3. buy a house

 _____

4. look for another job

 _____

5. get married

 _____

6. go to evening school

 _____

7. get a college degree

 _____

8. settle down

 _____

9. study more English

 _____

10. take a trip

 _____

Exercise D: *Will*

Please think about when you will (or will not) do the following things. Write full sentences. Use **I will** or **I will not** at the beginning of each sentence.

Examples: speak English well
    I will speak English well in two years.

    take a trip
    I will not take a trip this summer.

1. buy a new car

 _____

2. finish college

_____

3. get a good job

_____

4. get married

_____

5. travel around the world

_____

6. start my own business

_____

7. be rich

_____

8. buy a house

_____

9. become famous

_____

10. go to graduate school

_____

Exercise E: Cohesion (Connection)

Please complete the following sentences. Take words from the list below. Use each one only one time. The words in the list connect the ideas of different parts of sentences or of different sentences.

after that	_also_	_then_
and	_so_	_that_
but	_first_	_because_

1. He is one of my friends and he is _____ my brother.
2. We go to school together, _____ we play soccer together.
3. I think _____ we are going to be friends for a long time.
4. Roberto plays soccer and baseball, _____ he stays in shape.
5. He is fairly outgoing, _____ he is very sensitive.
6. He worries about our parents _____ they work so hard.
7. Roberto has some future plans. _____, he is going to study physical education.
8. He is going to improve his English. _____, he is going to study science and physical education.
9. He is going to get a college degree. _____, I don't know what he is going to do.

Exercise F: Punctuation

Reading 2 is repeated below without *punctuation*. Please read through it and add *commas, periods, question marks,* and *exclamation points.* The grammar and the capital letters will help you. Go back to Reading 2 and check your work after you finish.

My Friend Roberto

Roberto is one of my good friends He is also my brother We go to school together and we play soccer together We live together We even share a bedroom Of course we also share our parents I think that we are going to be friends for a long time We will certainly be brothers for a long time

Roberto is 21 years old He is about 5 feet 9 inches tall His face is long and narrow His eyes are green His hair is dark brown He doesn't look very Italian He smiles a lot and usually has a friendly look on his face He isn't fat and he isn't thin His build is average He plays soccer and baseball so he stays in shape He doesn't like to dress up He likes to wear jeans and T-shirts

Roberto has a pleasant personality He is fairly outgoing but he is also very sensitive He worries about our parents because they work so hard He also worries about our grandparents because they are old Our grandfather is also ill Roberto often writes to both of them He is my older brother but my English is better than his He is a little sensitive about that too Roberto is crazy about strawberry ice cream and soccer

Roberto's future plans are not very definite First he is going to improve his English Then he is going to study science and physical education He wants to be a high school coach After that I don't know what he will do He has a girlfriend and he likes her very much Is he going to marry her I don't know but I hope so I want him to be happy He is a good person and a true friend

---

Notes and Questions on the Organization of Reading 2

Part A: Paragraphs

Reading 2 is a description of a person. There are four paragraphs. Read them again. Be sure that you see four paragraphs. Notice the differences in the content of the paragraphs. The following questions will help you understand the system of paragraphs in Reading 2.

1. Where do you begin to get details about Roberto? Why is the first paragraph there, then? What does it do?

2. What kind of details do you get in the second paragraph?

3. What information does the third paragraph give you? How is it different from the second paragraph?

4. What new information does the fourth paragraph give you? How does it serve as a conclusion?

A *conclusion* can repeat, summarize, emphasize, or add to the information in a composition. Sometimes it does a little of everything.

Part B: Order

The following questions and comments will help you understand the order of Reading 2.

1. What is the general topic of Reading 2? It is true that "Roberto" is the topic, but what is the more general topic?

2. That general topic is divided into two parts, or categories. What are they? (Look at the second and third paragraphs.)

3. Look at the second paragraph. Notice that the writer begins the physical description with the head and face (after giving age and height).

4. Is it possible to change the order of the two categories? Can "personality" come before "physical appearance"? Which order do you prefer?

A division of a general topic into subtopics, parts, or classes is called *classification.* Think of topics that you might classify. (There are many examples in science.) Next, go on to Model 2.

1. _____

2. _____

3. _____

4. _____

APRIL

5. _____

6. _____

7. _____

8. _____

9. _____

Model 2 (Description)

My Girlfriend, Maria

Maria Herrera is a great person. She is a friend from school. She is also my girlfriend. I hope that we are going to be friends for a long time.

Maria is 19 years old. She will be 20 in two months. She is about 5 feet, 3 inches tall. Her eyes are brown and her face is round. Her hair is brown and curly. She wears it long. She has a very pleasant smile and she always has a twinkle in her eye. She doesn't wear glasses. She always looks nice. She wears dresses and skirts to school because she goes to work in a department store after class. She can't wear jeans to work.

Maria has a wonderful personality. She is a serious person, but she also likes to have a good time. She likes people and she likes parties. She doesn't have much time for fun, but she is always ready for a party on Saturday night. Maria is very smart. She is a good student and she gets good grades. She knows a lot about politics and psychology. She likes to discuss these subjects, but she doesn't make other people feel inferior. She is patient and kind. All of these qualities make her a good salesperson in the hat department at Maison Blanche. Plus, she is crazy about hats!

Maria's future plans are a little uncertain. However, she thinks that she is going to get a bachelor's degree in psychology. Then, perhaps she will go on to graduate school. I am sure that she will be successful. I also hope that she is going to include me in her future plans!

Caption Writing

Please write a sentence under each picture on page 22 or in your notebook.

Composition 2

Instructions for Student's Composition

1. On 8¹/₂ x 11 inch loose-leaf notebook paper, write four paragraphs about a friend. Describe your friend. Give your composition a title.

2. Remember to indent and leave margins. Put the following information in your paragraphs:

PARAGRAPH 1.   Introduce your friend. How do you know him/her? What do you think of the friendship?

PARAGRAPH 2.   Describe your friend physically: age, color of hair, color of eyes, face, body, clothes, etc.

PARAGRAPH 3.   Describe your friend's personality.

PARAGRAPH 4.   Conclude with your friend's future plans. Give your feelings about your friend's future.

3. Take what you need from Model 2. Let it help you with grammar, vocabulary, and ideas.

4. Your composition should look like this:

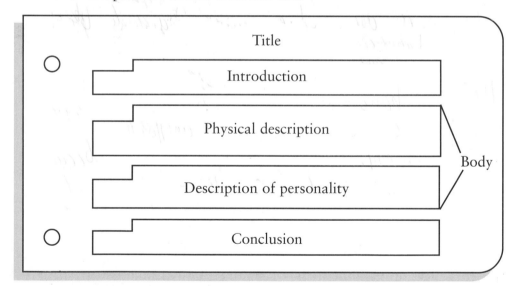

Connecting

Use a search engine (such as Netscape, Yahoo, or Excite). Type in the name of a famous person you like, such as a singer, writer, musician, or artist. What information can you find about this person. Tell a partner about the person.

Describing a Scene and Feelings

- **Composition Focus:** Friendly Letter in Conversational Tone Using Description and Narration

- **Organizational Focus:** Spatial Order (Second Paragraph)

- **Grammatical Focus:** Simple Past Tense
  There was/were
  Quantifiers, e.g., *most, all, several*

1. _____

2. _____

3. _____

4. _____

5. _____

6. _____

7. _____

8. _____

Reading 3

Before You Read

Think about this. Then talk about it with a partner.

Where were you yesterday? What did you do?
Do you feel *homesick* sometimes? When?

Read

A Letter to a Friend

February 12, 2002

Dear Carmen,

 It is early evening and I am sitting at home after a long day. It was not a nice day today and I felt homesick. I think of you often and all of my friends in Mexico. I miss everyone.

 It rained today here in New Orleans. Outside, the sidewalks were crowded with people. All of them wore coats and carried umbrellas. Everyone was in a hurry to get to a dry place. I hurried to work, too, because I forgot my umbrella. Buses and cars moved up and down the street. One of the cars went through a puddle of water and splashed me. I was upset about that, but inside the department store, it was warm and pleasant. I felt better then. As you know, I work in the hat department. Two elderly women were there this afternoon. One of them tried on funny hats. They both laughed and talked. I liked their New Orleans accents.

 Later, I went to a small restaurant close to work. There weren't many people there. There was just one young man at a small table near the window. I ate a piece of pecan pie. It tasted delicious. You know, the food in New Orleans is wonderful.

 I am fine. I am learning a lot in my classes. I like most of my teachers and classmates. One of my classmates is my new boyfriend. His name is Bruno and he is very nice. I attend classes every morning, I work every afternoon, and I study every evening. I don't have much free time, but I like my life in New Orleans.

 I hope that you are well and happy. How is school? How is your English? Can you read my letter? Please write soon. I enjoy your letters with news from home. My cousin, Sylvia, sends her regards.

Your friend,
Maria

After You Read

Caption Writing: Please write a sentence under each picture on page 26 or in your notebook.

Vocabulary from Reading 3

Find the words below in Reading 3. Examine the use of each word and see if you can guess the meaning. If you are not sure, ask a classmate or check your dictionary.

Nouns	**Verbs**	**Adjectives**
accent	carry	crowded
coat	forget	delicious
department store	hurry	dry
free time	laugh	funny
hat	miss	homesick
pecan pie	rain	upset
puddle	send	warm
regards	taste	wonderful
sidewalk	try on	
umbrella		**Expression**
	Adverbs	in a hurry
	down	
	early	
	up	

Sample Envelope

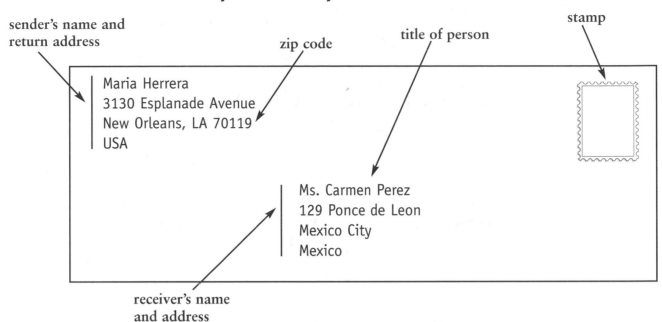

sender's name and return address

zip code

title of person

stamp

Maria Herrera
3130 Esplanade Avenue
New Orleans, LA 70119
USA

Ms. Carmen Perez
129 Ponce de Leon
Mexico City
Mexico

receiver's name and address

Exercise A: Addressing an Envelope

Please complete the envelope. Use your name and address for the sender's name and return address. Use the name and address of a relative or friend for the receiver.

Note to the student:
There are different ways to conclude or close a letter:

Love (when you write to a special friend or relative)
Sincerely (when you write a business letter or write to a friend)
Your friend (when you write to a friend)
Your cousin (when you write to a cousin)

Your teacher can explain other possibilities.

Exercise B: Simple Past Tense and *There was/were*

Part A

Please write the correct past tense form of the verbs to complete the sentences.

1. It _____ earlier today. (rain)

2. All the people _____ coats. (wear)

3. They _____ umbrellas. (carry)

4. I _____ to work. (hurry)

5. I _____ my umbrella. (forget)

6. A car _____ through a puddle and

    _____ me. (go, splash)

7. The women _____ and _____.
   (laugh, talk)

8. I _____ a piece of pie. (eat)

Part B

Please complete the sentences by writing *There was* or *There were* in the sentences below.

1. _____ many cars in the center of town.

2. _____ a young man in the restaurant.

3. _____ a flower on each of the tables.

4. _____ two elderly women in the department store.

5. _____ a small table near the window.

6. _____ many people walking on the sidewalks.

Exercise C: Quantifiers

Part A

Please complete the following sentences with the words of quantity below. Then look back and find each sentence in Reading 3 and check your answers.

everyone	*a lot*	*all of them*
most of	*all of*	*two*
one of them	*one of*	*every*
much		

1. I think of you often and _____ my friends in Mexico.

2. The streets were crowded with people. _____ wore coats and carried umbrellas.

3. _____ was in a hurry to get to a dry place.

4. _____ elderly women were there this afternoon.

5. _____ tried on funny hats.

6. I am learning _____ in my classes.

7. I like _____ my teachers and classmates.

8. _____ my classmates is my new boyfriend.

9. I attend classes _____ morning, I work _____ afternoon, and I study _____ evening.

10. I don't have _____ free time, but I like my life in New Orleans.

Part B

Look around you. Write sentences about the people and things around you using each of the quantifiers from Part A, above. Write the sentences in your notebook.

Exercise D: Spatial Terms

Part A

Please reread "A Letter to a Friend." Underline the **spatial terms.** These are the little words that tell you **where.** Then complete these sentences with the words from the list below. Make the meaning the same as in Reading 3.

up and down   *near*
in   *inside*
next to   *at*
close to   *outside*

1. I sat _____ a small restaurant.

2. The restaurant is _____ my work.

3. _____, the sidewalks were crowded with people.

4. Buses and cars moved _____ the street.

5. _____, it was warm and pleasant.

6. Nobody sat _____ me.

7. There was a young man _____ a small table.

8. His table was _____ the window.

Part B

Where were you last night? Think about it. Now write sentences using each of the spatial terms from Part A, above. Write about the people and things that were around you. Write the sentences in your notebook.

Exercise E: Spatial Order

Please reorganize the following groups of sentences. Number them in correct *order.* The order is according to *space.* (The information is not from Reading 3.)

A.

_____ There is a comfortable chair beside the table.

_____ As you enter the room, you will see a large table.

_____ In front of the chair, there is a small table.

_____ On the small table, there is a flower in a vase.

B.

_____ I am having lunch in the restaurant.

_____ Next to the window sit two pretty girls.

_____ There is a restaurant near my school.

_____ I am sitting near the window.

C.

_____ In the back of the room, there are also windows.

_____ Near the center of the room, there are many small desks.

_____ I study in a pleasant classroom.

_____ In the front of the room, there are large windows.

D.

_____ Near the children, there is a small fountain.

_____ There are trees and flowers around me.

_____ Under the trees, children are playing.

_____ I am sitting in a park.

E.

_____ I am a waitress in a small restaurant.

_____ It is warm and pleasant inside.

_____ People are walking in the snow.

_____ Outside, it is snowing.

Notes and Questions on the Organization of Reading 3

Part A: Paragraphs

Reading 3 is a friendly letter. "Friendly" means that it is not a business letter. The form of a business letter is different. (See Unit 6.) Reading 3 has five paragraphs. Go back to Reading 3. Be sure that you see five paragraphs. Notice the date, the name of the receiver of the letter, and the name of the writer of the letter. The following questions will help you understand the system of paragraphs in Reading 3.

1. The first paragraph describes something. What does it describe? Does it give a detailed or general description? Why do you think Maria begins that way?

2. What information does the second paragraph give? Does it give more description? What is the subject of the second paragraph? Will this description give Carmen a "picture" of Maria's daily life?

3. What does Maria describe in the third paragraph?

4. What information does Maria give in the fourth paragraph? How does this add to the "picture" of Maria's daily life?

5. What does the fifth paragraph do? Why is it last? Who is it about?

Is there really an *introduction,* a *body,* and a *conclusion* in a friendly letter? Is it the same as Reading 1 or Model 1? It isn't really, is it?

Part B: Order

Let's look at the second paragraph in Reading 3. The following questions will help you understand the *order* of the second paragraph. Remember that the word *order* refers to what is first, what is second, etc.

1. What is the place? Does Maria begin with details or with general information?

2. Does Maria describe the outside or the inside first? Why?

3. Where does the description of the inside begin?

4. Does Maria describe the furniture inside? The color of the walls? How does she describe the inside?

If the description tells "where," the writer is using *space order* or *spatial order.* Think of different descriptions that might need *spatial order.*

Notice these *spatial terms* in Reading 3:

in	*inside*
close to	*at*
outside	*through*
up and down	*near*

Think of other words for space. Ask your teacher for help. Next, go on to Model 3.

1. _____

2. _____

3. _____

4. _____

5. _____

6. _____

7. _____

8. _____

Model 3 (Friendly Letter)

A Letter to a Relative

July 9, 2002

Dear Dominick,

    It is Saturday evening and I am sitting in Audubon Park. It was a hot summer day in New Orleans. I am sitting under a huge oak tree and I am thinking of you.

    Earlier today the park was crowded with people. Many of them strolled through the park. There were many children on the playground. They played on the swings and ran around. Roberto and some friends played soccer. They wanted me to play, but it was too hot. Several of the friends were classmates from Lake College. The others were friends from our neighborhood in New Orleans. All of them went home a little while ago. They are good friends, but I prefer our friends from the old neighborhood in Rome. New friends are not the same, are they?

    I am fine, but I miss you and my other old friends. You are a good cousin and a good friend! I enjoy my classes and I am learning a lot. Most of my classmates are nice. One of my classmates is especially nice. She is also very pretty. Her name is Maria and she is my new girlfriend! I attend classes five mornings a week and I work at a music store three afternoons a week. I like my job.

    How are you? I hope you are well and happy. How is San Francisco? Roberto and I hope to visit you again soon. When will you come to New Orleans for a visit? I want you to meet Maria. Roberto says to tell you "Hello." Please write soon. Try writing in English!

Your cousin,
Bruno

Caption Writing

Please write a sentence under each picture on page 36 or in your notebook.

Composition 3

Instructions for Student's Composition

1. Write a letter to a friend or relative. Write on your own personal stationery, or on a piece of 8¹/2 x 11 inch loose-leaf notebook paper. Make it a real letter. Address the front of an envelope to put the letter in.

2. Follow the form for a friendly letter. Write four paragraphs. Remember to indent and leave margins. Put the following information in your paragraphs:

    PARAGRAPH 1.   Describe where you are. What are you doing?
    PARAGRAPH 2.   Talk about where you were earlier today and what other people did.
    PARAGRAPH 3.   Talk about your daily life.
    PARAGRAPH 4.   Talk about the person you are writing to.

    Then, conclude the letter with *Sincerely* or some other appropriate conclusion. Sign the letter with your first name only.

3. Take what you need from Model 3. Let it help you with the form of your letter, grammar, vocabulary, and ideas.

4. Your letter should look like this:

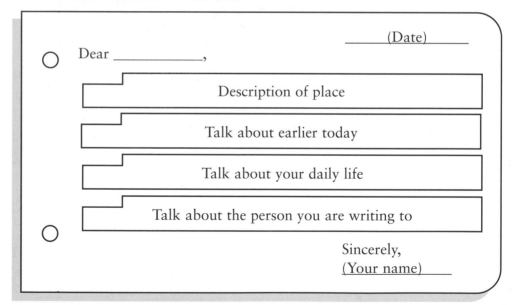

Connecting

Use a search engine (such as Netscape, Yahoo, or Excite). Look for department stores and places to go shopping in your city or local area. What hours are they open? What types of things do they sell? What other information can you find? Tell a partner about the stores.

Giving Instructions/ Directions

🎈 **Composition Focus: Process Description**

🎈 **Organizational Focus: Chronological Order**

🎈 **Grammatical Focus: Imperatives**
Modals: *can, should, will, might, may, must*

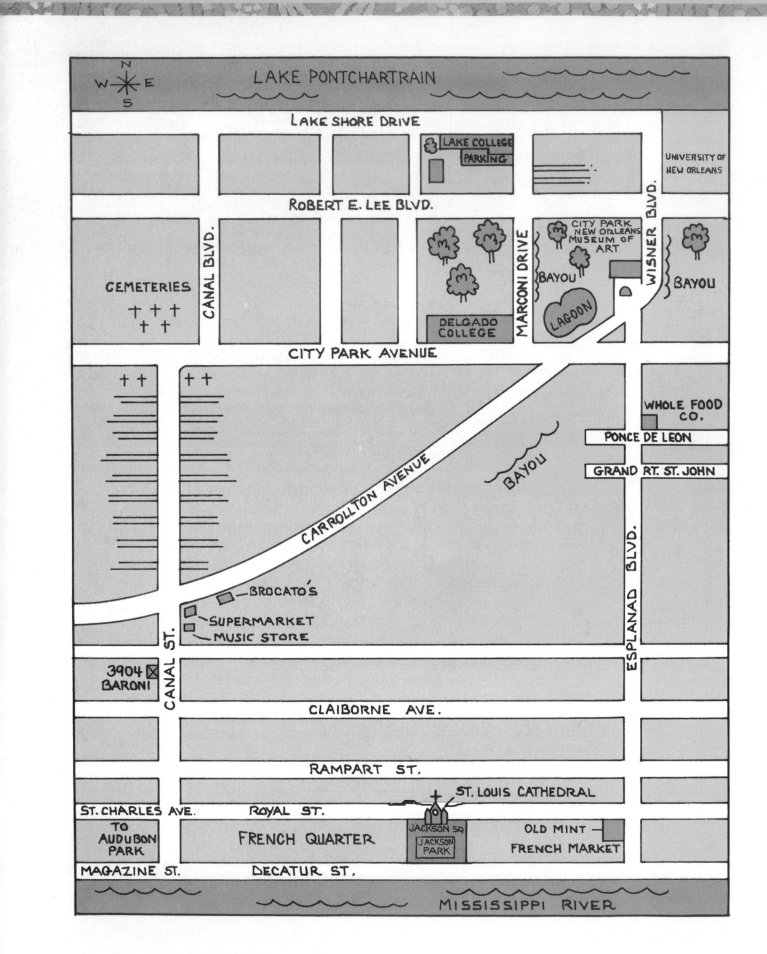

Reading 4

Before You Read

Think about this. Then talk about it with a partner.

Look at the map on page 40. Find the *intersection* of Robert E. Lee Boulevard and Canal Boulevard.

Find the *location* of these places: Lake College, 3904 Canal Street, St. Louis Cathedral, the Whole Food Company, Brocato's. What other places do you see?

Read

A Party

Some people like to give parties, but everyone likes to go to them. Giving a party can be fun. It can be easy and inexpensive, too, if all of the guests bring something to eat or drink. Bruno and Roberto are going to have a party next Saturday night. Here are the directions to their house.

> ### We are going to have a party this Saturday at 8:00 P.M.!
>
> Follow these directions to get to our house. They will lead you from Lake College to our house by car. You can find your way there from your house if you know the location of Lake College.
>
> From the parking lot of the school, turn right on Marconi Drive. Stay on Marconi until the first traffic light, then turn right again. This is Robert E. Lee Boulevard. Stay on Robert E Lee for about three blocks. At the corner of Robert E. Lee and Canal Boulevard, turn left. Canal is a long street and you will need to stay on it for about a mile. At the cemeteries, Canal Boulevard will become Canal Street. At that point, you must veer right and then veer left. Be careful here. This intersection can be very dangerous. You should stay on Canal Street for ten or twelve more blocks. Stop when you get to 3904 Canal Street. This is the place. Ring the bell and someone will let you in.
>
> We hope that you will come. Bring something to eat or drink. You may also bring a friend. You might miss a good time if you don't come.
>
> *Roberto and Bruno Baroni*

After You Read

Following Directions: Please draw a line on the map to show the way from Lake College to Bruno and Roberto's house.

Vocabulary from Reading 4

Find the words below in Reading 4. Examine the use of each word and see if you can guess the meaning. If you are not sure, ask a classmate or check your dictionary.

Nouns	**Verbs**	**Adjectives**
bell	become	careful
block	bring	dangerous
cemetery	follow	easy
corner	lead	inexpensive
directions	ring	
guest	stop	
intersection	turn	
location	veer	
mile		
parking lot	**Adverbs**	
point	left	
traffic light	more	
	right	

Exercise A: Imperatives

Please list all of the *simple imperatives* (no subject, no auxiliary) in Reading 4.

Example: *Follow these directions.*

1. _____

2. _____

3. _____

4. _____

5. _____

6. _____

7. _____

8. _____

9. _____

Exercise B: Modals

Please rewrite each of the following sentences. Use the *modal auxiliary* in parentheses. After you finish, check your sentences with the same sentences in Reading 4.

Example: Someone lets you in. (will)
Someone will let you in.

1. Giving a party is fun. (can)

   _____

2. It is easy and inexpensive, too. (can)

   _____

3. The directions lead you from Lake College to our house. (will)

   _____

4. You find your way there from your house. (can)

   _____

5. You need to stay on Canal Boulevard for about a mile. (will)

   _____

6. At the cemeteries, Canal Boulevard becomes Canal Street. (will)

   _____

7. The intersection is dangerous. (can)

   _____

8. There, you veer right and then left. (must)

   _____

9. You stay on Canal Street for ten or twelve more blocks. (should)

   _____

10. You bring a friend. (may)

   _____

Exercise C: Cohesion (Reference)

The italicized part of each sentence below refers the reader to another point of information. All of the sentences come from Reading 4. What is being referred to? Please circle the letter below the sentence to show the correct reference.

1. Some people like to give parties, but everyone likes to go to *them*.
   What does *them* refer to?

   a. some people

   b. everyone

   c. parties

2. Giving a party can be fun. *It* can be easy and inexpensive, too, if all of the guests bring something to eat or drink.
   What does *it* refer to?

   a. giving a party

   b. something to eat

   c. something to drink

3. We are going to have a party next Saturday night. Here are the directions to *our* house.
   What does *our* refer to?

   a. Bruno's

   b. Roberto's

   c. Bruno and Roberto's

4. Follow these directions. *They* will lead you from Lake College to our house by car.
   What does *they* refer to?

   a. the directions to Bruno and Roberto's

   b. Bruno and Roberto

   c. the students at Lake College

5. Canal is a long street and you will need to stay on *it* for about a mile.
   What does *it* refer to?

   a. a long street

   b. Canal Boulevard

   c. a mile

6. At the cemeteries, Canal Boulevard will become Canal Street. *At that point,* you must veer right and then veer left.
   What does *at that point* refer to?

   a. where people are buried

   b. where Canal Boulevard becomes Canal Street

   c. where Canal Boulevard starts

Exercise D: Chronological and Logical Order

Please reorganize the following groups of sentences. Number them in the correct *order*. This order is according to *time* and *logic*.

A.

_____ First, leave the parking lot at Lake College.

_____ At that traffic light, turn right.

_____ You will now be on Robert E. Lee Boulevard.

_____ It is three blocks from the parking lot to the first traffic light.

B.

_____ At the cemeteries, veer right and then left.

_____ At the corner of Robert E. Lee and Canal Boulevard, turn left on Canal.

_____ Drive along Canal until you get to the cemeteries.

_____ Stay on Robert E. Lee for about three blocks.

C.

_____ Drive along Canal Street for another ten or twelve blocks.

_____ This is the place!

_____ At the cemeteries, Canal Boulevard will become Canal Street.

_____ Stop when you get to 3904 Canal Street.

D.

_____ Please come and bring a friend.

_____ You have the directions to Bruno and Roberto's house.

_____ If you follow these directions, you can find your way there.

_____ You might also bring something to eat or drink.

Notes and Questions on the Organization of Reading 4

Part A: Paragraphs

Reading 4 describes how to do something. "How to" is a process. Therefore, Reading 4 is called a "process" description. There are three paragraphs in Reading 4. The following questions will help you understand the system of paragraphs.

1. Where does the process begin?

2. What does the first paragraph do, then? Where does the reader get the topic of the composition? How does the writer lead to it?

3. Where do the directions end? In other words, where does the process stop?

4. What does the last paragraph do?

The first paragraph usually introduces the topic, or subject, of the composition. Therefore, it is called the *introduction*. It leads the reader to the main part.

Part B: Order

Let's look at the second paragraph in Reading 4. The following questions and comments will help you understand the order.

1. Should the partygoer leave the parking lot before or after driving down Marconi Drive?

2. Which is first—driving west on Robert E. Lee or south on Canal Boulevard?

3. Does the partygoer drive down Canal Boulevard before or after veering right and left onto Canal Street?

4. The order is time, isn't it? Is the time order first to last or last to first? Notice the time words in the second paragraph.

5. If the process is described in the second paragraph, is time necessary in the first and third paragraphs? Why not?

Process descriptions usually need time order. Think of other kinds of topics that might use time order. Next, go on to Model 4.

1. _____

2. _____

3. _____

4. _____

5. _____

6. _____

7. _____

8. _____

10. _____

Model 4 (Process Description)

Bruno's Cheese Pie

I like to cook. I think that I am a good cook. Everyone in my family says so. I like to cook Italian food, but my favorite recipe is one from Maria, my Mexican girlfriend. This recipe is for cheese pie. I am preparing it for the party tonight. Here is the recipe.

First, butter the bottom of a round baking dish. Then, put flour tortillas around the bottom. Let them come up the sides of the dish, too. Next, chop one large tomato, one small can of chili peppers, and one onion. Put the chopped tomato, peppers, and onion on the tortillas. After that, beat together 3 eggs, 3 tablespoons of flour, 1 teaspoon of salt, $^1/_2$ teaspoon of baking powder, and $^1/_2$ cup of milk. Then, you should fold in 1 cup of grated cheese. Next, pour the mixture into the dish over the chopped tomato, peppers, and onion. Finally, put the dish in the oven. Don't cover the dish. Bake the cheese pie for 45 minutes at 350 degrees. The pie will serve 4 people.

After you take the pie out of the oven, you will need to let it cool for about 30 minutes. Arrange slices of avocado in a circle on the top of the pie. Add a few spoonfuls of taco sauce. Cut it in wedges and serve it to your guests. They will enjoy it.

Caption Writing

Please write a sentence under each picture on page 48 or in your notebook.

Composition 4

Instructions for Student's Composition

1. On 8^1/$_2$ x 11 inch loose-leaf notebook paper, write a composition. Tell someone how to do or make something. You might write out a recipe or tell someone how to build something. Give your composition a title.

2. Write three paragraphs. Remember to indent and leave margins. Put the following information in your paragraphs:

   PARAGRAPH 1.   Introduce your idea. What are you talking about? Can people use it?

   PARAGRAPH 2.   Describe the process. What comes first? What is second? What is next?

   PARAGRAPH 3.   What is the end of the process? Conclude with some general points.

3. Take what you need from Model 4. Let it help you with grammar, vocabulary, and ideas.

4. Your composition should look like this:

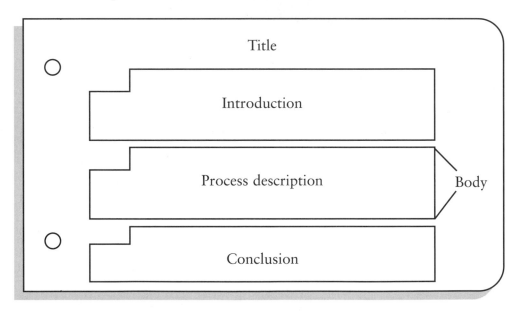

Connecting

Use a search engine (such as Netscape, Yahoo, or Excite). Type in "recipes." Look for a recipe that sounds interesting to you. Tell a partner about it.

Describing Past Events

- Composition Focus: Narration

- Organizational Focus: Chronological Order

- Grammatical Focus: Simple Past Tense
               Objects: Direct and Indirect

1. _____

2. _____

3. _____

4. _____

5. _____

6. _____

7. _____

8. _____

9. _____

10. _____

11. _____

Reading 5

Before You Read

Think about this. Then talk about it with a partner.

Look at the pictures on page 52. Find someone who is *angry, exhausted, nervous, happy,* and *upset.*
When do you feel *angry? Nervous? Upset? Happy? Exhausted?*

Read

Mrs. Baroni's Day

Friday was not a typical day for Mrs. Baroni, Roberto and Bruno's mother. It was difficult and frustrating. In the morning, she was late for work. In the afternoon, her boss got angry with her. By evening, she was exhausted. She is glad that most days are different.

At 6:00, the alarm clock rang and Mrs. Baroni got up as usual. She took a shower and then went straight to the kitchen. There, she fixed breakfast for her husband and her sons. After breakfast, her husband left for work, Bruno cleaned up the kitchen, and she got dressed. At 7:30, she said good-bye to Bruno and Roberto as they left for school. They drove to school. Then, she left the house and walked to the bus stop. So far, so good! She waited and waited at the bus stop. The bus finally came—about twenty minutes late. Then, on its way downtown, the bus broke down. All of the passengers had to get off and wait for another bus to come. Mrs. Baroni thought about her work, and she felt so nervous! Finally, she arrived at her office—thirty minutes late. Her boss wasn't very happy! Mrs. Baroni worked hard all morning. Then, at noon, she met some friends for lunch.

In the afternoon, her boss really got angry at her. Because she was upset in the morning, she forgot to mail an important form to the IRS (Internal Revenue Service). Friday was the deadline for the form. When her boss found out late in the afternoon, he said some very nasty things. Mrs. Baroni felt terrible. Later, her boss apologized. He knows that she really is a wonderful and valuable employee.

By the time Mrs. Baroni got home, she was exhausted. She told her family the whole story and they were very understanding. Bruno and Roberto offered to fix dinner while she took a long, hot bath. After her bath and a nice dinner, she felt much better. She went to bed early, while Bruno and Roberto did their homework. Mrs. Baroni really deserved a good night's sleep.

After You Read

Caption Writing: Please write a sentence under each picture on page 52 or in your notebook.

Vocabulary from Reading 5

Find the words below in Reading 5. Examine the use of each word and see if you can guess the meaning. If you are not sure, ask a classmate or check your dictionary.

Nouns	**Verbs**	**Adjectives**
bath	apologize	angry
boss	break down	difficult
deadline *termin*	deserve *zasługi*	exhausted *wyhoínosh*
employee *pracownik*	fix	frustrating
form	get off	glad
IRS (Internal Revenue Service)	think	hot
	wait	important
passenger		nervous
shower	**Adverbs**	terrible *okropny*
way	downtown	typical
	finally	understanding
	late	valuable *cenny*
	later	

Exercise A: Vocabulary

Please complete the following sentences with words from the list.

passengers   *typical*   *boss*   *frustrating*   *nervous*
deserved   *late*   *employee*   *exhausted*   *apologized*

1. Friday was very different. It was not _____typical_____.
2. Friday was not a good day. It was difficult and _____frustrating_____.
3. The bus was not on time. It was twenty minutes _____late_____.
4. All of the _____passengers_____ on the bus were angry.
5. Mrs. Baroni was very worried and _____nervous_____.
6. At work, her _____boss_____ asked about the IRS form.
7. He was angry and said some bad things, but later he _____apologized_____.
8. Mrs. Baroni works hard and she is a good _____employee_____.
9. After a long day at work, Mrs. Baroni was _____exhausted_____.
10. After such a bad day, Mrs. Baroni _____deserved_____ something nice.

Exercise B: Simple Past Tense

Please reread Reading 5. Look for verbs in the simple past tense and underline them. Then, please change these sentences about Mrs. Baroni to the *past*. Change the verb to the simple past tense. If there is a present time word, change it to a past time word.

Example: Every morning, Mrs. Baroni goes to work.
Yesterday morning, Mrs. Baroni went to work.

1. Every day, Mrs. Baroni gets up at 6:00.

   Yesterday Mrs Baroni got up at 6.00

2. Every morning, her alarm rings at 6:00.

   last morning Yesterday, her alarm rang at 6:00

3. Mrs. Baroni gets up and takes a shower.

   Mrs Baroni got up and took a shower

4. After her shower, she fixes breakfast.

   After her shower, she fixed breakfast

5. After breakfast, she gets dressed.

   After breakfast she got dressed

6. Roberto and Bruno leave for school at 7:30.

   Roberto and Bruno left for school at 7 30

7. They drive to school.

   They drove to school

8. Mrs. Baroni walks to the bus stop and waits for the bus.

   It walked to the bus stop and waited

9. She gets to work at 8:00.

   She got to work at 8.00

10. Then, she has a cup of coffee and starts her work.

    she had a cup of coffee and started her

11. At noon every day, Mrs. Baroni meets her friends for lunch.

    at noon Mrs Baroni met her friends for lun

12. Some afternoons, she works until 5:30.

    last afternoons she worked until 5.30

13. Every evening, Mrs. Baroni eats dinner with her family.

    Yesterday Mrs Baroni ate dinner with her fam

14. Some evenings, Bruno cooks dinner for everyone.

    last evening Bruno cooked dinner for everyone

Exercise C: Objects

Please answer the following questions with information from Reading 5. Pay attention to the position of the *objects*.

1. What did Mrs. Baroni do after she took a shower?

   _____

2. Who did she fix breakfast for?

   _____

3. Where did Mr. Baroni go after breakfast?

   _____

4. Where did Bruno and Roberto go at 7:30?

   _____

5. Where did Mrs. Baroni walk to after she left the house?

   _____

6. How long did she wait for the bus?

   _____

7. Where did the bus break down?

   _____

8. Where did she finally arrive thirty minutes late?

   _____

9. What did Mrs. Baroni forget to do in the morning?

   _____

10. When did the boss find out?

    _____

11. When did Mrs. Baroni feel better?

    _____

Exercise D: Chronological Order

Please reorganize the following groups of sentences. Number them in correct **time order**. (Another name for time order is **chronological order**.)

A.

___3___ In the afternoon, her boss got angry with her.

___4___ By evening, she was exhausted, but she relaxed a little.

___1___ Friday was not a typical day for Mrs. Baroni.

___2___ In the morning, she was late for work.

B.

___2___ After she got up, she took a shower.

___3___ After her shower, she went to the kitchen.

___1___ Mrs. Baroni's alarm clock rang at 6:00.

___4___ Then, she fixed breakfast.

C.

___2___ After they left, Mrs. Baroni walked to the bus stop.

___1___ At 7:30, Mrs. Baroni said good-bye to Roberto and Bruno.

___4___ The bus came, and Mrs. Baroni got on it.

___3___ She waited for the bus.

D.

___3___ After lunch, Mrs. Baroni went back to work.

___1___ At noon, Mrs. Baroni met some friends for lunch.

___2___ They went to a restaurant near her office.

___4___ Then, she worked hard until 5:00.

Exercise E: Capitalization

Reading 5 is repeated below without capital letters. Please read through it and add capital letters. The grammar and punctuation will help you. Afterwards, go back to Reading 5 and check your work.

Mrs. Baroni's Day

friday was not a typical day for mrs. baroni, roberto and bruno's mother. it was difficult and frustrating. in the morning, she was late for work. In the afternoon, her boss got angry with her. by evening, she was exhausted. she is glad that most days are different.

at 6:00, the alarm clock rang and mrs. baroni got up as usual. she took a shower and then went straight to the kitchen. there, she fixed breakfast for her husband and her sons. after breakfast, her husband left for work, bruno cleaned up the kitchen, and she got dressed. at 7:30, she said good-bye to bruno and roberto as they left for school. they drove to school. then, she left the house and walked to the bus stop. so far, so good! she waited and waited at the bus stop. the bus finally came—about twenty minutes late. then, on its way downtown, the bus broke down. all of the passengers had to get off and wait for another bus to come. mrs. baroni thought about her work, and she felt so nervous! finally, she arrived at her office—thirty minutes late. her boss wasn't very happy! mrs. baroni worked hard all morning. then, at noon, she met some friends for lunch.

in the afternoon, her boss really got angry at her. because she was upset in the morning, she forgot to mail an important form to the irs (internal revenue service). friday was the deadline for the form. when her boss found out late in the afternoon, he said some very nasty things. mrs. baroni felt terrible. later, her boss apologized. he knows that she really is a wonderful and valuable employee.

by the time mrs. baroni got home, she was exhausted. she told her family the whole story and they were very understanding. bruno and roberto offered to fix dinner while she took a long, hot bath. after her bath and a nice dinner, she felt much better. she went to bed early, while bruno and roberto did their homework. mrs. baroni really deserved a good night's sleep.

Notes and Questions on the Organization of Reading 5

Part A: Paragraphs

Reading 5 tells a kind of story. It is the story of someone's daily life. The writer explains Mrs. Baroni's daily life by explaining a day in the past. There are four paragraphs. You might expect five paragraphs: an introduction, "morning," "afternoon," "evening," and a conclusion. Look carefully to understand the organization of Reading 5. Look to see how it is divided into paragraphs. The following questions will help you understand the system of paragraphs in Reading 5.

1. In the first paragraph, how does the writer divide the day?

2. Is the second paragraph about the morning?

3. What is the third paragraph about?

4. Where do you get information on the afternoon? On the evening?

5. How is the conclusion different from the other readings? The conclusion of the day is the conclusion of the composition, isn't it?

Sometimes, the **conclusion** of a composition is the end of the main part, or *body*. In Reading 5, the last part of the body also serves as the conclusion.

Part B: Order

By now, you probably understand the order of Reading 5. The following questions will help you to be sure.

1. How much time does the second paragraph cover?

2. How much time does the third paragraph cover? Is this time before or after the time in the second paragraph?

3. How much time does the last paragraph cover? Is the time before or after the time in the third paragraph?

4. Look for time words. Is the order from early to late or from late to early?

Remember that this kind of order is called *time order*, or *chronological order*. It is almost automatic to use time order in a composition on daily activities. Next, go on to Model 5.

1. _____

2. _____

3. _____

4. _____

5. _____

6. _____

7. _____

8. _____

9. _____

10. _____

11. _____

Model 5 (Narration)

Bruno's Day

Yesterday was a typical day for Bruno. It was long and tiring, but it was interesting. In the morning, he went to class. In the afternoon, he went to work. In the evening, he had dinner with his family and studied. That is the way his life goes.

Bruno jumped out of bed at 6:00 and did some exercises. Then, he took a shower, shaved, and brushed his teeth. After he got dressed, he went to the kitchen for breakfast. His mother had it ready for him. As he ate his toast and fruit, he thought about his girlfriend, Maria. After breakfast, he cleaned up the kitchen and did the dishes while his mother got ready for work. At 7:30, he and his brother, Roberto, were ready to leave for school.

Traffic was light, so Bruno and Roberto drove to school in fifteen minutes. Roberto went straight to class and Bruno went to the library. He asked the librarian some questions and looked up some information for his chemistry class. Then, he rushed to the cafeteria to meet Maria before their nine o'clock class. After his eleven o'clock class, he met Roberto and Roberto's girlfriend, Sylvia, for lunch. He couldn't have lunch with Maria because she doesn't finish her class until 1:00. By that time, he has to go to work.

The rest of the day passed as usual. After lunch, Roberto dropped Bruno off at the music store where he works. Bruno sold a clarinet, two guitars, and a violin before the afternoon was over. He got off work at 5:30 and took the bus home. Nobody was home when he arrived, so he started dinner. Spaghetti was ready and on the table when his parents and Roberto got home. They were hungry and ready to eat! After dinner, Bruno relaxed for a few minutes and then started his homework. He studied until midnight and fell into bed. He was asleep before his head hit the pillow. It was a typical day!

Caption Writing

Please write a sentence under each picture on page 60 or in your notebook.

Composition 5

Instructions for Student's Composition

1. On 8½ x 11 inch loose-leaf notebook paper, write a composition about yesterday or another past day. Describe the day. Give your composition a title.

2. Write four paragraphs. Remember to indent and leave margins. Put the following information in your paragraphs:

   PARAGRAPH 1.   What kind of day was it? What was your main morning activity? What was your main afternoon activity? What was your main evening activity? How did you feel by evening?

   PARAGRAPH 2.   Describe your morning (early).

   PARAGRAPH 3.   Describe the next part of your day.

   PARAGRAPH 4.   Describe the rest of your day. Conclude with bedtime.

3. Take what you need from Model 5. Let it help you with grammar, vocabulary, and ideas.

4. Your composition should look like this:

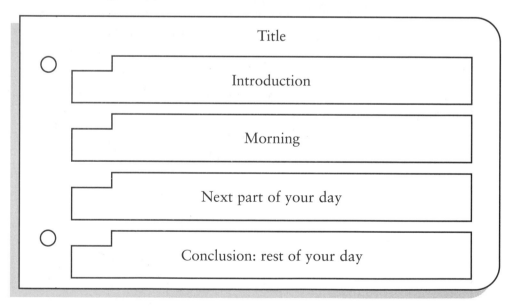

Connecting

Use a search engine (such as Netscape, Yahoo, or Excite). Can you find any information about the IRS (the Internal Revenue Service)? Tell a partner what you found.

Making a Written Request

POSITIONS AVAILABLE

EXECUTIVE ASSISTANT position available with Greater New Orleans Tourist Commission. Must have excellent skills: word processing, shorthand, computer. Send references and resume to GNOTC, 529 St. Ann Street, New Orleans, LA 70116

- Composition Focus: Business Letter

- Organizational Focus: Ranking of Requests

- Grammatical Focus: Imperatives
  Polite Requests with *would*

1. _____

2. _____

3. _____

4. _____

5. _____

6. _____

7. _____

8. _____

9. _____

10. _____

11. _____

12. _____

Reading 6

Before You Read

Think about this. Then talk about it with a partner.
What *skills* do you have? Can you *type*? Do *word processing*?
Use a *computer*? *Take shorthand*?
What kind of job would you like to have?

Read

A Business Letter

3904 Canal Street
New Orleans, LA 70119
March 19, 2002

Greater New Orleans Tourist Commission
529 St. Ann Street
New Orleans, LA 70116

Dear Madam/Sir:

I would like to request an interview for the position of executive assistant. I saw your advertisement in Friday's Times Picayune. I can type 80 words a minute. I can take shorthand at 120 words a minute. I am able to use many computer programs for word processing and spreadsheets. I can also speak three languages: English, Italian, and Spanish. I have a diploma from a business institute in Rome, Italy. I worked for five years at the Italian Tourist Commission in Rome. I arrived in the New Orleans area four years ago. Now, I am working as a bilingual assistant for a large corporation downtown. I am interested in changing jobs. My English is good and my skills are excellent. I am also a responsible employee.

I would like to work for the Greater New Orleans Tourist Commission. I enjoyed my work with the tourist commission in Rome and I would like to return to that kind of office. I would be happy to give you a list of references and a complete resumé of my work experience.

Please contact me at the above address. Thank you very much.

Sincerely,
Sophia Baroni

After You Read

Caption Writing: Please write a sentence under each picture on page 64 or in your notebook.

Vocabulary from Reading 6

Find the words below in Reading 6. Examine the use of each word and see if you can guess the meaning. If you are not sure, ask a classmate or check your dictionary.

Nouns	Verbs	Adjectives
advertisement	change	bilingual
business institute	contact	complete
computer program	request	excellent
corporation	type	responsible
diploma		
executive assistant		
interview		
language		
position		
reference		
resumé		
shorthand		
skill		
spreadsheets		
tourist commission		
word processing		
work experience		

Exercise A: Comprehension

Please reread Reading 6. Then, answer the following questions to check your *comprehension.* Go back to Reading 6 if you have trouble.

1. Where does Sophia Baroni live?
   a. 529 St. Ann Street
   b. Rome, Italy
   c. 3904 Canal Street
   d. Times Picayune

2. When did Sophia Baroni write the letter?
   a. Four years ago
   b. Five years ago
   c. Friday
   d. March 19, 2002

3. What is the zip code of the Greater New Orleans Tourist Commission?
   a. 70116
   b. 529
   c. 70119
   d. 3904

4. Why did Sophia Baroni write to the Greater New Orleans Tourist Commission?
   a. She wanted to improve her typing skills.
   b. She wanted to interview for a job.
   c. She once worked for the Italian Tourist Commission.
   d. She enjoyed her work in Rome.

5. What are Mrs. Baroni's skills?
   a. She can speak English.
   b. She can type, take shorthand, and use a computer.
   c. She is a responsible employee.
   d. She has a diploma from a business institute.

6. What is Mrs. Baroni's work experience?
   a. She has a diploma from a business institute in Rome.
   b. Her English is good, her skills are excellent, and she is a responsible employee.
   c. She worked in Rome for five years and she is with a large corporation in New Orleans now.
   d. She arrived in New Orleans four years ago and found a job soon after that.

Exercise B: Vocabulary/Comprehension

Please answer these questions about yourself.

1. Where do you live?

   I live in Glen Cove

2. What is your zip code?

   My zip code is 11542

3. What is the zip code for your school?

   My school's zip code is 10021

4. Do you work now? If so, what is the name of your workplace?

   Yes I do

5. What is the name of a company you would like to work for?

   I would like to work for US Army or IT company.

6. What skills do you have?

   _____

7. What is your work experience?

   _____

Exercise C: Indirect Requests with *would + like to*

Please rewrite the following sentences. Change *want to* to *would like to*. *Would like to* is more polite. It means *allow me* or *permit me* when you direct it to someone. It is an indirect request.

Example: I want to request an interview.
                I would like to request an interview.

1. I want to apply for a job.

   _____

2. I want to receive an application.

   _____

3. I want to get a diploma from a business institute.

   _____

4. I want to work in the admissions office.

   _____

5. I want to study English at Lake College.

   _____

6. I want to work for Shell Oil Company.

   _____

7. I want to be a typist in your office.

   _____

8. I want to show you my references.

   _____

9. I want to send you a resumé of my work experience.

   _____

10. I want to thank you.

   _____

Exercise D: Direct Requests

Part A

Please write one request for each of the following situations. Use the *imperative* with *please*. Use *me, to me,* or *for me* in each request. Use the verb in parentheses.

> *Example:* You have a question. You need an answer. (answer)
> *Please answer a question for me.*

1. You need an application form. (send)

   _____

2. You need some information. (get)

   _____

3. You want to know the rules. (explain)

   _____

4. You need a college catalog. (send)

   _____

5. You want to receive a phone call or letter. (contact)

   _____

6. You want to receive a letter at your home address. (write)

   _____

7. You want to know the schedule. (tell)

   _____

8. You know the answer. You want someone to ask a question. (ask)

   _____

9. You want to understand the problem. (explain)

   _____

10. You want to hear the news. (tell)

    _____

Part B

Please rewrite each request from Part A. Use **Would you please** to make a polite direct request.

    Example: You have a question. You need an answer. (answer)
                       Would you please answer a question for me?

1. _____

2. _____

3. _____

4. _____

5. _____

6. _____

7. _____

8. _____

9. _____

10. _____

Exercise E: Ranking

Please reorder the information on the right below. Rank it from most to least or least to most. Let your teacher help you decide on the "logic."

1. Population of U.S. Cities

Chicago, Illinois	2,721,547	_____
Los Angeles, California	3,553,638	_____
New York, New York	7,380,906	_____
Houston, Texas	1,744,058	_____

2. U.S. Postal Service Insurance

Insurance	Fee	
$200.01 to $300	$3.70	_____
$100.01 to $200	$2.75	_____
$0.01 to $50	$0.85	_____
$50.01 to $100	$80	_____

3. Principal Islands of the World

	Area (square miles)	
Madagascar	226,657	_____
Borneo	290,320	_____
New Guinea	341,631	_____
Greenland	839,999	_____

4. Telephone Numbers in New Orleans

Weather	(504) 525-8831	_____
Emergency (Police/Fire/Medical)	911	_____
Time	(504) 529-6111	_____
Travelers' Aid	(504) 525-8726	_____

Notes and Questions on the Organization of Reading 6

Part A: Paragraphs

Reading 6 is a business letter. Notice that the form is a little different from the friendly letter in Unit 3. Look at the differences. There are three paragraphs in Reading 6, in addition to the other parts (addresses, names, etc.). The following questions will help you understand Reading 6. The system of paragraphs in a business letter is different from that in a regular composition.

1. Does the first paragraph lead the reader to the main part in the second paragraph? If not, what does it do?

2. Is the second paragraph the main part, or body? If not, what is it? What does the reader get in the second paragraph?

3. What does the last paragraph do? What is last in the last paragraph?

A letter is different from a composition. A letter has a kind of *conclusion,* but the *introduction* and *body* are not the same. There is no separate introduction. The writer begins the letter with the main point.

Part B: Order

The following questions will help you understand the *order of information* in Reading 6.

1. What does the writer request in the first paragraph? Why is the other information there?

2. What is the second paragraph about? How does that information connect to the first paragraph? What is the point of the second paragraph?

3. What does the writer request in the third paragraph?

4. Of the three paragraphs, which contains the most central point? How important are the other points, or requests?

Think of other kinds of writing where you might *rank* information. Ranking means to prioritize (to put in order of importance: first, then second, then third, etc.). Writers often rank statistical information, such as the population of cities. How is ranking different from time order? Ask your teacher to explain. What might be a reason for ranking? With cities, for example, which one probably goes first? How do you decide? Next, go on to Model 6.

1. _____

2. _____

3. _____

4. _____

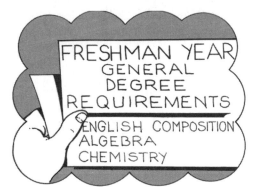

5. _____

6. _____

7. _____

8. _____

A Business Letter

3904 Canal Street
New Orleans, LA 70119
July 25, 2002

Admissions Office
University of New Orleans
Lakefront Campus
New Orleans, LA 70148

Dear Madam/Sir:

Please send me an application for admission to the University of New Orleans. I have a diploma from Warren Easton High School in New Orleans. Now, I am taking general undergraduate courses at Lake College. This year, I completed my freshman courses in English composition, algebra, and chemistry. Next year, I will complete more general degree courses. I would like to begin my studies at the University of New Orleans in two years. My major field of interest is music.

I would also like to receive information on tuition and financial aid for students. Are there any special scholarships for music majors? In addition, I would like to know more about the course requirements for a degree in music. I hope that my courses at Lake College will transfer to UNO.

Please send all of this information as soon as possible. It will help me plan my courses at Lake College for the next school year. Please send the information to the above address. Thank you very much.

Sincerely,
Bruno Baroni

Caption Writing

Please write a sentence under each picture on page 74 or in your notebook.

Composition 6

Instructions for Student's Composition

1. Write a business letter to a company or an institution. Write on $8^1/2$ x 11 inch paper. Address an envelope for the letter.

2. Follow the form for a business letter. Write your address and the date in the top right corner. To the left, 1 inch down, write the name and address of the person who will receive the letter. Under that, $^1/4$ inch down, write *Dear Madam, Dear Sir,* or *Dear* __(full name)__.

3. Write three paragraphs. Remember to indent and leave margins. Put the following information in your paragraphs:

   PARAGRAPH 1.   What do you want? Tell about yourself (if appropriate).
   PARAGRAPH 2.   Add any other requests or information.
   PARAGRAPH 3.   When do you want an answer? Say thank you.

   Conclude with *Sincerely* or *Sincerely yours.* Sign your full name.

4. Take what you need from Model 6. Let it help you with the form of your letter, grammar, vocabulary, and ideas.

5. Your letter should look like this:

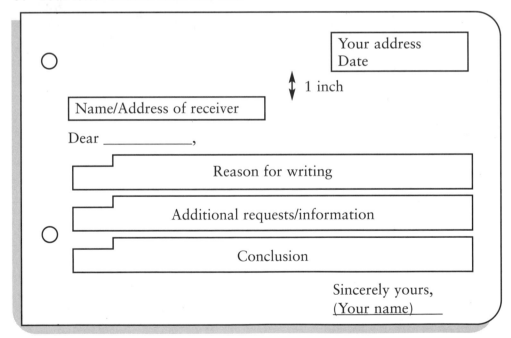

 # Connecting

Use a search engine (such as Netscape, Yahoo, or Excite). Can you find any lists of job openings? Tell a partner what you found.

Describing Past Events

🍭 **Composition Focus:** Narration

🍭 **Organizational Focus:** Chronological Order

🍭 **Grammatical Focus:** Simple Past Tense
Past Continuous Tense
Predicate Infinitives (*to* + verb)

1. _____

2. _____

3. _____

4. _____

5. _____

6. _____

7. _____

8. _____

Reading 7

Before You Read

Think about this. Then talk about it with a partner.

Did you ever miss a plane, bus, or train? If so, why did you miss it?
Did you ever have a bad trip? Where did you go? What happened?

Read

A Terrible Trip

My brother, Roberto, and I took a trip to Miami last summer. I will never forget it. We have some cousins in Miami and they wanted us to visit them. We thought about the beautiful beaches, so we decided to go. We also wanted to see our cousins, Angelo and Gina.

We had reservations on an early flight to Miami, so we got up before the sun rose. Roberto and I were all excited about the trip. Our father got up early to drive us to the airport. While we were driving to the airport, we had a flat tire! This made us miss our flight and it made our father late for work. As Roberto and I were waiting around the airport for another flight, we tried to call our cousins. Unfortunately, they weren't at home. They were on their way to the Miami Airport to pick us up! We finally boarded a flight and arrived in Miami four hours late. Of course, our cousins were not at the airport to meet us. We called their house and asked them to come back to the airport. They were very understanding. We waited outside for them, and after a half hour, they drove up. When we saw them, we were so relieved! We apologized and apologized for all the trouble and inconvenience.

We stayed for a week and had a terrible time. It wasn't our cousins' fault, but nothing went right. It rained every day and we didn't go to the beach even one time. On the second day, while we were playing tennis, Gina fell and hurt her leg. For the rest of the week, she couldn't walk. Then, Angelo had a car accident while he was driving us around the city. We weren't hurt, but the car was in the repair shop for the rest of the week.

When it was time to leave, we were both sad and happy. We wanted to return home, but we hated to leave Angelo and Gina.

We said good-bye and begged them to visit us in New Orleans. We wanted to try again for a smooth visit. We had to take a taxi to the airport because their car was still in the shop. You will never guess what happened next! Yes, while we were going to the airport, the taxi broke down. Fortunately, someone stopped to help and drove us to the airport. We arrived just in time to catch our plane. When we landed in New Orleans, our parents were at the airport to meet us. They couldn't believe our story!

After You Read

Caption Writing: Please write a sentence under each picture on page 78 or in your notebook.

Vocabulary from Reading 7

Find the words below in Reading 7. Examine the use of each word and see if you can guess the meaning. If you are not sure, ask a classmate or check your dictionary.

Nouns	Verbs	Adjectives
accident	beg	flat
beach	board	relieved
cousin	catch (a flight or plane)	smooth
fault	decide	
flight	guess	
inconvenience	hurt	
repair shop		
reservation	**Adverbs**	
tire	fortunately	
	unfortunately	

Exercise A: Simple Past Tense

Please reread Reading 7 and look for verbs in the *simple past tense.*
Underline them. Then, answer the questions about the story using past
tense verb forms.

1. When did Roberto and Bruno take a trip to Miami?

   _____

2. At what time did Roberto and Bruno get up for their flight to Miami?

   _____

3. Why did they miss their flight?

   _____

4. When did they arrive in Miami?

   _____

5. Did they have a good time in Miami?

   _____

6. How long did Roberto and Bruno stay with their cousins?

   _____

7. Why didn't they go to the beach?

   _____

8. Why couldn't Gina walk?

   _____

9. Why was the car in the repair shop?

   _____

10. What happened to the taxi on the way to the airport?

   _____

Exercise B: Past Continuous Tense

Please write the *past continuous* form of the verb in parentheses to tell what was happening at the same time as another past action.

Example: While we **_were playing_** tennis, Gina fell. (play)

1. Mr. Baroni _____ his sons to the airport when a tire went flat. (drive)

2. While Bruno and Roberto _____ for a flight, they tried to call their cousins. (wait)

3. While they _____ to call, their cousins were on their way to the airport. (try)

4. Gina _____ tennis when she fell and hurt her leg. (play)

5. While Angelo _____ a left turn, he had an accident. (make)

6. The taxi arrived while Roberto _____ good-bye. (say)

7. Someone stopped to help while Roberto and Bruno

   _____ next to the taxi. (stand)

8. Mr. Baroni _____ home when Roberto told him about the terrible trip. (drive)

Exercise C: Simple Past Tense vs. Past Continuous Tense

Please write the correct form of the verb: simple past tense or past continuous tense. Use the past continuous in the *while* clause. Use the simple past tense in the rest of the sentence.

> *Example:* While it __*was raining*__ , we __*watched*__ a movie. (rain, watch)

1. While Gina _____, we _____ a game. (rest, play)

2. We _____ around the airport when we

    _____ a loud noise. (walk, hear)

3. While Roberto _____, Bruno _____ at a magazine. (call, look)

4. While Angelo and Gina _____ lunch, the phone

    _____. (eat, ring)

5. It _____ every day while they _____ their cousins. (rain, visit)

6. While they _____ down the road, a car

    _____ them. (drive, hit)

7. While they _____, Gina _____ them a gift. (pack, give)

8. While they _____ to some music, Gina's friends

    _____ to the house. (listen, come)

9. The rain _____ while they _____ to the airport. (stop, go)

Exercise D: Predicate Infinitives

Combine each group below. Write only one sentence for each group. Every verb after the first one in each sentence should be in the *infinitive form* with *to.*

Example: They wanted us. We came. We visited them.
They wanted us to come to visit them.

1. We decided. We went.

   _____

2. We wanted. We saw our cousins, Angelo and Gina.

   _____

3. Our father got up. He drove us to the airport.

   _____

4. We called our cousins. We told them about the flight.

   _____

5. We asked them. They came back to the airport.

   _____

6. We ran. We greeted them.

   _____

7. After a week, it was time. We left.

   _____

8. We hated. We left our cousins.

   _____

9. We got into a taxi. We went to the airport.

   _____

10. Someone stopped. Someone helped.

    _____

11. We arrived just in time. We caught our plane.

    _____

Exercise E: Cohesion (Connection)

Please reread Reading 7. Look for *words that connect* a subject and verb to another subject and verb. (Sometimes the second subject is not repeated.) Underline these connecting words: *and, so, because, when, but.* Then, combine each of the following groups of sentences below. Use the connecting words in parentheses. Be careful with word order, punctuation, and capital letters. Write a total of twelve sentences.

> *Example:* We went to Miami. (but)
> We had a terrible trip.
> *We went to Miami, but we had a terrible trip.*

1. We have some cousins in Miami. (and)
   They wanted us to visit them.

   _____

   _____

2. We thought about the beautiful beaches. (so)
   We decided to go.

   _____

   _____

3. We had reservations on an early flight. (so)
   We got up. (before)
   The sun rose.

   _____

   _____

4. We tried to call our cousins. (but)
   They weren't at home.

   _____

   _____

5. We finally boarded a flight. (and)
   We arrived in Miami four hours late.

   _____

   _____

6. We saw them. (when)
   We were so relieved!

   _____

   _____

7. It wasn't our cousins' fault. (but)
   Nothing went right.

   _____

   _____

8. Angelo wasn't hurt in the accident. (but)
   Their car was in the repair shop for the rest of the week.

   _____

   _____

9. It was time to leave. (when)
   We were both sad and happy.

   _____

   _____

10. We had to take a taxi to the airport. (because)
    Their car was still in the shop.

    _____

    _____

11. Someone stopped to help. (and)
    Someone drove us to the airport.

    _____

    _____

12. We landed in New Orleans. (when)
    Our parents were at the airport to meet us.

    _____

    _____

Notes and Questions on the Organization of Reading 7

Part A: Paragraphs

Reading 7 tells the story of someone's trip. By now, you already know the system of paragraphs to expect. The following questions will guide you.

1. In which paragraph does the trip begin? What information comes before that point? What is the name of the paragraph leading to the main point?

2. In which paragraph does the trip end? How many paragraphs long is the body, then?

3. Is there a separate conclusion? There isn't, is there?

The system of paragraphs in Reading 7 is the same as in Reading 5. The end of the trip (in Reading 5, the end of the day) is the end of the composition. In other words, the last part of the *body* is the *conclusion.* This often happens when we write about a period of time.

Part B: Order

By now, you probably don't need questions to help you see when the *order of information* is *chronological.* Check the time words in Reading 7. Look again to see how the time is divided. In other words, where in the composition do you get the arrival and the departure? Where do you find information about the time in between? Next, go on to Model 7. See if it is organized the same way.

1. _____

2. _____

3. _____

4. _____

5. _____

6. _____

7. _____

8. _____

9. _____

Model 7 (Narration)

A Memorable Trip

I took a fantastic trip with my family when I was ten years old. I remember it well. My aunt, uncle, and cousins were living on a little farm in the country outside Rome and they invited us to visit them. These cousins, Angelo and Gina, are the same cousins who live in Miami now. Our trip to visit them a long time ago was very different from our recent trip to Miami.

It was a Saturday morning when we left home. We got up early that morning before the sun rose. We were sleepy, but we were excited and ate breakfast quickly. We left home at 5:30 in order to get an early start. It took us three hours to get there in my father's old car. When we arrived at the house, my father honked the horn to announce our arrival. Everyone ran out to greet us. We all hugged and kissed each other.

We stayed for two days and had a marvelous time. We played outside all day and helped Uncle Vito feed the chickens. He taught us how to make wine. He also showed us how to play checkers. At night, Roberto and I played checkers with Angelo and Gina while listening to the grown-ups tell stories about their childhood.

When it was time to leave, we were very sad. My mother was especially sad to leave my Aunt Rosalina, her sister. They begged us to stay longer, but we had to leave. My father had to go to work the next day. As I look back, that trip was a long, long time ago. Aunt Rosalina and Uncle Vito are both dead, and Gina and Angelo are living in Miami. The world is different now.

Caption Writing

Please write a sentence under each picture on page 88 or in your notebook.

Composition 7

Instructions for Student's Composition

1. On 8^1/$_2$ x 11 inch loose-leaf notebook paper, write a composition about a trip. Give details of the trip. Perhaps the trip was good, or perhaps the trip was bad. Give your composition a title.

2. Write four paragraphs. Remember to indent and leave margins. Put the following information in your paragraphs.

   PARAGRAPH 1.   Where did you go? When did you go? Why did you go?
   PARAGRAPH 2.   Tell about the beginning of the trip.
   PARAGRAPH 3.   How long did you stay? What did you do?
   PARAGRAPH 4.   Tell about coming home. Tell about your feelings.

3. Take what you need from Model 7. Let it help you with grammar, vocabulary, and ideas.

4. Your composition should look like this:

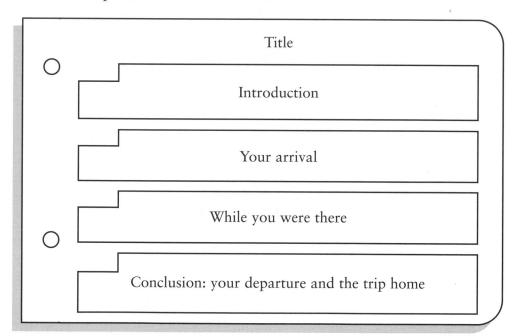

 # Connecting

Use a search engine (such as Netscape, Yahoo, or Excite). Imagine you are planning a trip. Choose a destination and find airplane flights to that place from an airport near your city or town. What airlines offer flights? How much are the fares? What times do the flights leave? Tell a partner about the information you find.

Describing Seasons and Weather

🍭 **Composition Focus: Exposition**

🍭 **Organizational Focus: Classification**

🍭 **Grammatical Focus: Simple Present Tense**
Present Perfect Tense

1. _____

2. _____

3. _____

4. _____

5. _____

6. _____

7. _____

8. _____

9. _____

10. _____

11. _____

Reading 8

Before You Read

Think about this. Then talk about it with a partner.

Look outside. What is the *weather* like today? What is the *temperature*? What *season* is it? Which season do you like the most: *spring, summer, fall,* or *winter?* Why?

Read

The Weather in Chicago

The weather is important to everyone. It is more than the subject of conversation. People's lives and moods change with the weather. My family and I have visited our friend, Salvatori, in Chicago several times in the summer, but we have never visited him in the winter. It's December now, and here we are in Chicago. We have been here for two weeks. It's much colder in Chicago than in New Orleans at this time of year. In Chicago and this part of the United States, there are definitely four seasons: winter, spring, summer, and fall.

This winter has been very unpleasant. It has snowed a lot and people have had trouble with their cars. Last night, it snowed. Now there are two feet of snow on the ground. This has been fun for Bruno and me but Salvatori didn't have fun this morning when his car got stuck in the snow. In fact, since morning many people have gotten stuck in the snow. Schools have closed because students couldn't get to school. Many people have stayed inside. When people do go outside, they need to wear heavy coats, boots, hats, and gloves. It has gotten very, very cold. Salvatori says that the temperature has dropped to 0° Fahrenheit and below! Brrr!

According to Salvatori, spring and fall are lovely seasons here. In the springtime, everything comes alive. The snow melts, the grass turns green, and flowers begin to bloom. People seem happy and spend more time outside. The sun shines almost every day. Salvatori says that the leaves turn orange, yellow, and red in the fall. The weather is still warm and pleasant. People drive to the country in order to see the fall colors. This is our friend's favorite season.

Summer is a good season in the north-central part of the United States, too. Our last visit was in the summertime. It gets hot and humid, but there are fun things to do. Salvatori says he goes on picnics, swims a lot, and gives parties in his backyard. He relaxes and takes life easier. It sometimes rains here, he says, but that is not a problem. After the rain is over, the air is cool and pleasant.

People's lives certainly change with the weather. My life would be different in Chicago. I'm glad that I don't live here. Our friend, Salvatori, likes Chicago, but he isn't crazy about winter, either.

After You Read

Caption Writing: Please write a sentence under each picture on page 92 or in your notebook.

Vocabulary from Reading 8

Find the words below in Reading 8. Examine the use of each word and see if you can guess the meaning. If you are not sure, ask a classmate or check your dictionary.

Nouns	**Verbs**	**Adjectives**
fall	melt	cold
mood	shine	cool
season	snow	heavy
snow	stick	humid
spring		unpleasant
summer	**Adverb**	warm
temperature	definitely	
weather		**Expression**
winter		Brrr!

Exercise A: Verbs for Weather

Please choose *verbs* from the following list to complete the sentences below. Use each verb only one time. The grammar and the meaning will help you decide. Every sentence says something about the *weather* and the *seasons* of the year in the northern part of the United States.

snows	*turns*	*rains*
gets	*are*	*fall*
drops	*comes*	*shines*
bloom		

1. In the springtime, the grass _____ green.

2. Flowers _____ in the spring.

3. The sun _____ almost every day in the summertime.

4. In the fall, leaves _____ from the trees.

5. In the spring, everything _____ alive.

6. In the winter, the temperature _____ to zero.

7. It sometimes _____ and we need to carry umbrellas.

8. It _____ very, very cold in the winter.

9. It _____ a lot in the winter and children like to throw snowballs.

10. There _____ four seasons: spring, summer, fall, and winter.

Exercise B: Expressions for Weather

Please rewrite each of the following sentences two times. Use *becomes* and *gets* in place of *is.* At the end of each sentence, use *in the (season)*. (Fill in the word that is best for your climate.) Every sentence says something about the *weather.*

> *Example:*   It is warm.
> *It becomes warm in the spring.*
> *It gets warm in the spring.*

1. It is cool and pleasant.

   _____

   _____

2. It is hot and humid.

   _____

   _____

3. It is cold and rainy.

   _____

   _____

4. It is sunny.

   _____

   _____

5. It is hot and dry.

   _____

   _____

6. It is dark and cloudy.

   _____

   _____

7. It is cool and foggy.

   _____

   _____

Exercise C: Simple Present Tense (Third Person Singular)

Please complete the following sentences. They tell about people's activities in the summer. Use the *simple present tense*. Begin each sentence with *In the* _____ *time, everyone* _____. Be careful with the third-person singular verb form.

> *Example:*   go to the beach
> *In the summertime, everyone goes to the beach.*

1. go swimming

   _____

2. spend a lot of time outside

   _____

3. sit in the sun

   _____

4. go on picnics

   _____

5. have parties outside

   _____

6. relax

   _____

7. take life easy

   _____

8. listen to music in the yard

   _____

9. drive to the country

   _____

10. seem happy

    _____

Exercise D: Present Perfect Tense

Please write the *present perfect tense* for the verbs in parentheses to show actions which have continued from past to present. Use *has/have* + past participle.

> *Example:* It _*has rained*_ for three days. I hope it will stop soon. (rain)

1. Salvatori _____ four days of school because of the snow. (miss)

2. He _____ a lot of snow this winter. (see)

3. Many people _____ to Florida for the winter this year. (go)

4. We _____ our friends in California several times. (visit)

5. The weather _____ hot and humid all this week. (be)

6. We _____ good weather today, but tomorrow it will be bad. (have)

7. In Chicago, they _____ some warm weather. (get)

8. My parents _____ with our friends in Chicago several times. (stay)

9. They _____ their visits in the fall. (enjoy)

10. Finally, it's spring! The snow _____. (melt)

Exercise E: Present Perfect Tense

Please answer each question with a complete sentence. Use the *present perfect tense* in your answers.

> *Example:* Have you ever been to Chicago?
> *Yes, I have been to Chicago.* OR
> *No, I have not been to Chicago.*

1. Have you ever built a snowman?

   _____

2. Have you ever gotten stuck in the snow?

   _____

3. Has the school ever closed because of snow?

   _____

4. Has the weather been nice this week?

   _____

5. Has the weather been cold this week?

   _____

6. Has it snowed yet this year?

   _____

Exercise F: Word Order

Please rewrite the following sentences. Change the *word order*. Put the last part of each sentence first. Don't forget to use a comma after each part that you put first.

> *Example:* There are four seasons in the northern part of the United States.
> *In the northern part of the United States, there are four seasons.*

1. Everything comes alive in the springtime.

   _____

2. The sun shines almost every day in the summertime.

   _____

3. The leaves turn orange and red in the fall.

   _____

4. It gets hot and humid in the summer.

   _____

5. The air is cool and pleasant after the rain is over.

   _____

6. It snows a lot in the wintertime.

   _____

7. It gets very, very cold in the winter.

   _____

8. People need to wear heavy coats when they go outside.

   _____

9. There are different activities for each season.

   _____

10. There are four seasons in Chicago.

    _____

Notes and Questions on the Organization of Reading 8

Part A: Paragraphs

In Reading 8, the writer explains the weather in a certain region. In Chicago, where the writer's friend lives, there are four seasons. Therefore, you might expect six paragraphs: an introduction, one paragraph for each season, and a conclusion. However, there are only five paragraphs. The following questions will help you understand the system of paragraphs in Reading 8.

1. Where does the writer introduce the topic? How does the writer introduce the topic?

2. Where does the writer explain each season? Does the writer combine any seasons in order to explain? If so, how?

3. Where does the writer end the explanation of the seasons? Is this the end of the body, then? What follows?

4. How does the writer conclude the composition? How does he begin the conclusion?

You can see that there are three basic parts in Reading 8: an *introduction* (the first paragraph), a *body* (the three following paragraphs), and a *conclusion* (the last paragraph). This is the usual system of paragraphs in composition writing, although the number of paragraphs can vary. The paragraphs form the three basic parts. Be sure that you understand the system. Be sure that you understand how the paragraphs can form these parts and work together.

Part B: Order

The following questions will help you understand the order of information in Reading 8.

1. Does the writer explain the organization of the topic "weather"? How? Where?

2. How many subtopics, or classes, does the writer give you?

3. Does the writer give equal space to each subtopic?

4. Which season is explained first? Which ones follow? Is another order possible? Why does the writer talk about winter first?

In Unit 2, you learned about *classification*. It is a division into subtopics, or classes. *Weather* is a good topic to classify. Can you think of others? Next, go on to Model 8.

1. _____

2. _____

3. _____

4. _____

5. _____

6. _____

7. _____

8. _____

9. _____

Model 8 (Exposition)

The Weather in New Orleans

The weather! The weather! The weather! Don't people talk about anything else? It is true that the weather is important to us. Our activities and moods change with the weather. As the seasons change, our lives may become easy or difficult. My family and I have lived in New Orleans for four years and we've visited other parts of the United States. New Orleans is different from some other parts of the United States. Here, we don't really have four seasons. We have summer, and then there is the rest of the year!

Summertime is a hot and humid time. The hot weather lasts from May to October. Many people turn on their air conditioners and stay indoors. The sun shines, except when it rains. It rains often, but it becomes hot and humid again right after the rain. People carry umbrellas for the rain and the sun! Summertime is also a fun time, especially for young people. This summer, my brother, Roberto, and I have often gone with our friends to the Gulf Coast to spend the day on the beach. We usually take a picnic lunch and swim or sit in the sun. Since June, the beaches have been especially crowded on the weekends. In the evening sometimes, we have listened to music on the lakefront, gone out to eat with our girlfriends, or taken them to a movie. Summer nights in New Orleans are usually warm and romantic. I love summer!

Fall, winter, and spring are really one big season. It rains a little, but it never snows. In December and January, the temperature is cool, but it rarely freezes. When it doesn't freeze, flowers bloom all year round. My mother loves that! She especially loves the month of April. That's when the azaleas and camellias bloom. Everyone in our family is very busy in fall, winter, and spring. My brother and I work part time and study full time. My parents work long hours.

The weather is important to all of us. Our lives change with the weather. Summer is the best season for my family and me. We can relax and take life a little easy. I don't like the busy, busy times. Why can't we have summer all year long?

Caption Writing

Please write a sentence under each picture on page 102 or in your notebook.

Composition 8

Instructions for Student's Composition

1. On 8¹/2 x 11 inch loose-leaf notebook paper, write a composition about the weather in a familiar place. Organize the weather into seasons. Describe the seasons. Give your composition a title.

2. Write four, five, or six paragraphs. The number of paragraphs depends on how you choose to organize your writing. You can combine seasons that are similar. Remember to indent and leave margins. Put the following information in your paragraphs:

   FIRST PARAGRAPH.   Introduce the topic. Is the weather important? Which part of the world are you writing about? How many seasons are there?

   PARAGRAPHS 2, 3 (4, 5).   Describe the seasons.

   LAST PARAGRAPH.   Conclude with general statements. What are your opinions?

3. Take what you need from Model 8. Let it help you with grammar, vocabulary, ideas, and organization.

4. Your composition should look like this:

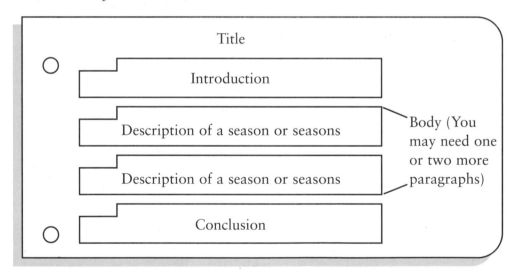

 # Connecting

Use a search engine (such as Netscape, Yahoo, or Excite). Make a list of cities you would like to visit. Then see if you can find the average winter and summer temperatures for each of the cities. Which city on your list has the coldest temperature? Which city has the warmest temperature? Tell a partner about the information you've found.

Contrasting People and Personalities

🔍 **Composition Focus: Description**

🔍 **Organizational Focus: Classification**
              Balance of Contrasts

🔍 **Grammatical Focus: Modals**
              Two-Word Verbs

1. _____

2. _____

3. _____

ITALIAN?
MEXICAN?

SWEDISH?
DANISH?

4. _____

5. _____

6. _____

7. _____

8. _____

9. _____

Reading 9

Before You Read

Think about this. Then talk about it with a partner.

What do you look like?
Describe your *personality*. Are you *serious? Reserved? Social? Organized? Artistic?*

Read

Sylvia and Maria

Sylvia Gomez and Maria Herrera are very different. They look different and their personalities are different. Yet, they are cousins and roommates. They even date brothers. Maria is my girlfriend and Sylvia dates my brother, Roberto. Most people cannot believe that they are cousins. Some people cannot even believe that they are from the same country.

Sylvia is fairly tall with long, straight brown hair. Maria is short and she has long, curly black hair. Sylvia is quite thin. Both of them are very attractive. Maria has warm, dark brown eyes and a nice smile. Her smile melts my heart. Sylvia's light blue eyes are bright and beautiful. Most people think that Maria is Mexican or Italian. They say that Sylvia must be from Denmark or Sweden.

Their personalities are different, too. Both are very serious students, but Sylvia is quiet and reserved and Maria is not. Maria is not really loud, but she likes to go to parties and have fun. Maria is a social person. She likes to talk while Sylvia likes to listen. Maria likes to dance while Sylvia likes to watch people dance. Maria likes to turn on the TV and Sylvia likes to turn it off. Maria turns up the radio and Sylvia turns it down. Sylvia is very tidy and artistic. She loves colors and well-organized space. Maria, on the other hand, is not especially neat. She doesn't always put away her things or pick up her clothes. That upsets Sylvia. Yet, they both work hard to have a comfortable and attractive apartment.

Sylvia and Maria are very different, but they are very pleasant people. Their differences are surprising and interesting. They are good friends and they love each other very much. Roberto and I love them, too.

After You Read

Caption Writing: Please write a sentence under each picture on page 106 or in your notebook.

Vocabulary from Reading 9

Find the words below in Reading 9. Examine the use of each word and see if you can guess the meaning. If you are not sure, ask a classmate or check your dictionary.

Noun	Verbs	Adjectives
roommate	believe	artistic
	date	attractive
	pick up	comfortable
	put away	curly
	turn down	dark
	turn off	loud
	turn on	quiet
	turn up	reserved
		serious
Adverbs		social
especially		straight
fairly		surprising
		tidy
		well-organized

Exercise A: Vocabulary: Antonyms

Please find the *antonym* (the word with the opposite meaning). Write it below.

different	*straight*	*fat*
reserved	*· tidy*	*loud*
light	*ugly*	*messy*
attractive		

1. Maria is sometimes not *neat,* but Sylvia is never

   _____.

2. Maria is very *social,* while Sylvia is more _____.

3. Sylvia is tall and *thin,* but Maria is short and a little

   _____.

4. Maria's hair is *curly.* Sylvia's hair is _____.

5. Sylvia is very *quiet,* while Maria is sometimes _____.

6. Maria's eyes are *dark* in color. Sylvia's eyes are _____.

7. Maria and Sylvia live in the *same* apartment, but they take

   _____ _____ classes.

8. Sylvia thinks the colors blue and red are *beautiful,* but Maria thinks

   those colors are _____.

9. Maria thinks that she is *not pretty,* but she really is very

   _____.

10. Sylvia's room is always *well-organized,* but Maria's room is

    sometimes _____.

Exercise B: Modals

Please rewrite the following sentences. Use the *modal auxiliaries* in parentheses. Put them into your sentences. Make any necessary changes.

Examples: Most people *don't believe* that Maria and Sylvia are cousins. (cannot)
Most people cannot believe that Maria and Sylvia are cousins.

Maria and Sylvia *are* in different classes next year. (may)
Maria and Sylvia may be in different classes next year.

1. People *don't believe* that they are from the same country. (cannot)

   _____

2. They think that Sylvia *is* from Denmark. (might)

   _____

3. They say that Maria *is* Mexican or Italian. (must)

   _____

4. Maria's smile *melts* your heart. (will)

   _____

5. Maria *tells* you that she is fat. (will)

   _____

6. Sylvia *relaxes* a little because she is too serious. (should)

   _____

7. Because Sylvia is artistic, she *studies* art after she learns more English. (may)

   _____

8. Maria is a little loud. She *quiets* down. (should)

   _____

9. Sylvia and Maria *work* part time to earn money for food, rent, and tuition. (must)

   _____

10. Sylvia and Maria *don't go* to a movie after school because they *go* to work. (can't, must)

    _____

Exercise C: Modals

Please "translate" the *meaning* of the italicized part of each sentence below. Please circle the letter below the sentence to choose the correct translation.

1. Sylvia doesn't look Mexican. Some people think that she *might be* from Denmark. Others think that she *might be* from Sweden or Finland.

    a. probably is

    b. is possibly

    c. will be

2. Most people *cannot believe* that Maria and Sylvia are cousins.

    a. don't want to believe

    b. refuse to believe

    c. find it difficult to believe

3. Because Sylvia is artistic, she *may study* art after she finishes her English courses.

    a. will possibly study

    b. finds it easy to study

    c. has her parents' permission to study

4. Because Sylvia and Maria don't have much money, they *must work* to pay for food, rent, and tuition.

    a. like to work

    b. enjoy working

    c. have to work

5. Maria is so short that she *can't reach* the top of the bookcase.

    a. is unable to reach

    b. doesn't want to reach

    c. isn't smart enough to reach

6. Sylvia is a little too serious. She *should relax* more.

    a. has to relax

    b. finds it possible to relax

    c. ought to relax

7. Maria and Sylvia *will visit* their families in Mexico City next summer.

    a. are thinking about visiting

    b. are going to visit

    c. are hoping to visit

8. After Maria and Sylvia visit their families, they *may spend* some time in Acapulco.

    a. are going to spend

    b. have to spend

    c. will possibly spend

9. Sylvia and Maria plan to cook dinner for Roberto and Bruno. The refrigerator is empty. They *must go* shopping.

    a. find it absolutely necessary to go

    b. are thinking about going

    c. will possibly go

10. *Will* Maria and Sylvia *marry* Bruno and Roberto? Who knows!

    a. Do Maria and Sylvia want to marry them?

    b. Are Maria and Sylvia going to marry them?

    c. Do Maria and Sylvia have their parents' permission to marry?

Exercise D: Two-Word Verbs

Please rewrite each sentence or request below. Change the underlined *noun object* to a *pronoun object*. Separate the *two parts of the verb* and put the pronoun object between them. The two-word verbs are boldfaced.

Example: Please **turn down** <u>the radio</u>.
              Please turn it down.

1. Would you please **hand in** <u>your homework</u>?

   _____

2. You should **put away** <u>your notes</u> before the examination.

   _____

3. Will you please **turn up** <u>the TV</u>?

   _____

4. Could you please **fill out** <u>this form</u>?

   _____

5. **Throw away** <u>those old newspapers</u>, please.

   _____

6. You must **write down** <u>this telephone number</u>.

   _____

7. Please **pick up** <u>those pieces of paper</u>.

   _____

8. You should **look over** <u>these apples</u> before you buy them.

   _____

9. You should **turn on** <u>the news</u> now if you want to watch it.

   _____

10. Please **turn off** <u>that light</u> when you finish studying.

   _____

Exercise E: Two-Word Verbs

Please rewrite the sentences below. Rewrite only the sentences that need *two-word verbs*. Take out the italicized part and put in a two-word verb. The italicized part gives the *meaning*. Choose from the list of two-word verbs below. Use each verb only one time.

pick up	*put away*	*turn off*
fill out	*hand in*	*turn up*
write down	*throw away*	*turn down*
look over	*turn on*	

Example: I need to *lower the volume* on the radio. The baby can't sleep.
I need to turn down the radio.

1. I should *give* my homework *to the teacher*. She expects to have it before we leave class.

   _____

2. You must *note* all the important information. You will need to have it in your notebook in order to study for the examination.

   _____

3. You may *dispose of* these old shoes. I don't need them any more. They are no good.

   _____

4. You should *raise the volume* on the radio. I can't hear it.

   _____

5. Will you please *complete* this application? We need your name, address, and social security number.

   _____

6. You should *examine* your answers. Look for careless mistakes.

   _____

7. Would you please *start* the TV? It's time for the news.

   _____

8. Please *remove* these pencils *from the floor*. Someone might fall.

   _____

9. Please *stop* the radio. I can't sleep.

   _____

10. Children should learn to *place* their toys *in the proper spot* after they finish playing.

    _____

Notes and Questions on the Organization of Reading 9

Part A: Paragraphs

Reading 9 describes two people. There are four paragraphs. Look back at those paragraphs to identify the three basic parts: the *introduction, body,* and *conclusion.* The following questions will help you understand the system of paragraphs in Reading 9.

1. Where does the writer introduce the topic? What is it?

2. Where does the main part begin? Where does it end? How long is it? How is it divided?

3. Where does the conclusion begin? How does the writer conclude the composition? What does the writer do with the topic in the conclusion?

Part B: Order

Look back at the introduction to the composition. Do you know what kind of order to expect in the body of the composition? Does the writer tell you? The following questions will help you understand the order of information in Reading 9.

1. The specific topic is Sylvia and Maria. What kind of topic is that? How can that kind of topic be organized? (Do you remember Unit 3?) Into how many subtopics does the writer divide the topic? What are the subtopics?

2. Which subtopic comes first in the body of the composition? Which comes second? Does it matter? It doesn't really, does it?

Do you remember that this kind of organization is *classification*? In Reading 9, there is something else happening within each class, or subtopic. Look closely. Do you see *brown–black, tall–short, thin–fat,* etc.? Notice that each characteristic is followed by the opposite characteristic. There is a balance. Let's call it a *balance of contrasts*. Sometimes the contrasts are indirect. Pick out contrasts in the third paragraph. Next, go on to Model 9 to see the same techniques.

1. _____

2. _____

3. _____

4. _____

5. _____

6. _____

7. _____

8. _____

Model 9 (Description)

Roberto and I

My brother, Roberto, and I are different in many ways. We look different and our personalities are different. Of course, we are also similar in some ways, but the differences are probably more interesting.

I look like my mother's side of the family, but Roberto looks more like my father's. He is fairly tall with dark brown hair, almost black. I am shorter and my hair is light brown. His eyes are dark brown to match his hair, while mine are green. Roberto has a medium build and he is more athletic. I am a little jealous of his muscles. I try to stay in shape. My mother says that I eat too much. Yet, Roberto is the one who loves ice cream. Life is not fair!

Our personalities are different, too. I like music and can play the violin well. I can pick up a piece of music, look it over, and play it immediately. I also love playing drums in a band. Everyone says that I have a lot of musical ability. Roberto, on the other hand, has athletic ability. He loves soccer and is an excellent goalie. He also enjoys baseball. In college, he plans to major in physical education, while I plan to get a degree in music. In addition to our different abilities, I am more outgoing than Roberto. I love to be with people. Roberto isn't exactly shy, but he is a sensitive guy. He worries about our parents because they work so hard. He worries about our grandparents in Rome because they are old and Grandfather is ill. He also worries about his English. He is a little jealous of my English because mine is better. Yet, he is the big brother!

Our differences sometimes cause us problems. We sometimes argue and disagree. However, we love each other and accept our differences. We can't stay angry at each other for long. After all, we have to share a bedroom.

Caption Writing

Please write a sentence under each picture on page 116 or in your notebook.

Composition 9

Instructions for Student's Composition

1. On 8¹/2 x 11 inch loose-leaf notebook paper, write a composition about yourself and someone you know. Choose someone who is very different from you. Write about the differences. Give your composition a title.

2. Write four paragraphs. Remember to indent and leave margins. Put the following information in your paragraphs:

   PARAGRAPH 1.   What are you writing about? Who are you writing about? Say that you are dividing the topic into looks and actions. What do people think?

   PARAGRAPH 2.   Describe the differences in physical appearance.

   PARAGRAPH 3.   Describe the differences in personality.

   PARAGRAPH 4.   Conclude with general statements. Do the differences cause problems? How do you feel about the differences?

3. Take what you need from Model 9. Let it help you with grammar, vocabulary, ideas, and organization.

4. Your composition should look like this:

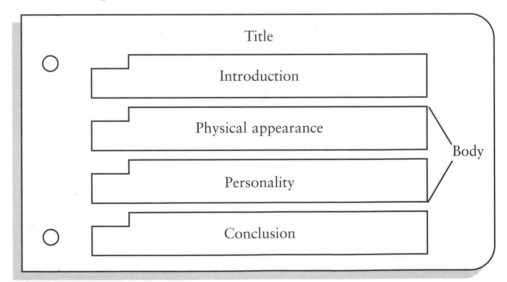

Connecting

Use a search engine (such as Netscape, Yahoo, or Excite). Choose a celebrity or famous person. Find information about the person. What differences are there between the person and yourself? Tell a partner how you and the person are different.

Recounting Experiences

MUSEUM

🔴 **Composition Focus: Exposition**

🔴 **Organizational Focus: Classification**

🔴 **Grammatical Focus: Present Perfect Tense**
Simple Past Tense vs. Present
Perfect Tense
Forms of Comparison

1. _____

2. _____

3. _____

4. _____

5. _____

6. _____

7. _____

8. _____

9. _____

Reading 10

Before You Read

Think about this. Then talk about it with a partner.

Where do you live now? How long have you lived there?
What do you like about the place? What things about the place seem strange to you?

Look at the pictures on page 120. Find the following places, things, and holiday celebrations in the pictures:

bayou   *Fourth of July*   *monument*   *cruise*
fireworks   *swamp*   *Thanksgiving*   *turkey*

Read

My Stay in New Orleans

My family and I arrived in the United States on March 4, 1998. We came here from Italy by plane. It was hard for us to leave our home and our relatives, but we wanted to make a new life here. Since that time, I have seen many curious and exciting places. I have also learned a lot.

New Orleans was very strange to me in the beginning. It was very different from Rome, my hometown. New Orleans seemed small and unexciting. I saw no grand buildings, wide boulevards, or ancient monuments. While some areas of town seemed clean and modern, others appeared old and dirty. Since then, I have become familiar with New Orleans and I like it better. I have visited the New Orleans Museum of Art and the Audubon Zoo. I have taken a river cruise on the Delta Queen. I have taken a boat tour of the bayous and swamps. I have become acquainted with the French Quarter and marvelous jazz music. I have eaten in splendid restaurants. Now I know that New Orleans is as exciting and alive as Rome. Now it seems charming and friendly to me.

When I first arrived, I felt so confused and lost because I didn't know any English at all. Since then, I have learned a lot of English. It has been difficult because Italian is very different from English. Italian grammar seems more regular and less idiomatic. Nevertheless, I speak English almost like a native now. I have also learned a lot about American culture and the unique history of New Orleans. Last November, my family ate Thanksgiving turkey with some American families. We have watched the fireworks over the Mississippi River

➡

on the Fourth of July for several years. Roberto and I have gone to some terrific jazz concerts at Preservation Hall. We have seen the site where Andrew Jackson defeated the British in the Battle of New Orleans. I still have a lot to learn, but I feel comfortable here now.

My family and I intend to stay in New Orleans forever. This is our new home. I hope to travel more in the future and visit all fifty states. I also hope to visit Italy soon to see my grandparents and all my old friends. I don't want them to forget me. I will never forget them.

After You Read

Caption Writing: Please write a sentence under each picture on page 120 or in your notebook.

Vocabulary from Reading 10

Find the words below in Reading 10. Examine the use of each word and see if you can guess the meaning. If you are not sure, ask a classmate or check your dictionary.

Nouns	Verbs	Adjectives
area	appear	acquainted
bayou	defeat	alive
cruise	intend	ancient
culture		charming
fireworks		confused
Fourth of July		curious
history		dirty
hometown		exciting
monument		familiar
native		grand
relative		idiomatic
site		lost
swamp		marvelous
Thanksgiving		modern
turkey		regular
		splendid
		strange
		terrific
		unexciting
		unique
		wide

Exercise A: Vocabulary

1. Please list the words that describe nice or interesting things in Reading 10.

   a. *exciting*_____   h. _____

   b. _____   i. _____

   c. _____   j. _____

   d. _____   k. _____

   e. _____   l. _____

   f. _____   m. _____

   g. _____   n. _____

2. Please list the words that describe bad or uninteresting things in the reading.

   a. _____   e. _____

   b. _____   f. _____

   c. _____   g. _____

   d. _____   h. _____

3. What are the words for types of waterways and wetlands found in the New Orleans area?

   a. _____   c. _____

   b. _____

4. Do any of these words describe the area where you live now? Which ones?

   _____

   _____

5. Do any of these words describe your hometown? Which ones?

   _____

   _____

Exercise B: Present Perfect Tense

Please answer the following question by completing the sentences below. Use the *present perfect tense* with *he has* + past participle.

Question
What has Bruno seen, done, or learned since he arrived in the United States?

Example: become acquainted with New Orleans
Since he arrived, he has become acquainted with New Orleans.

1. visit the New Orleans Museum of Art
He has visited the New Orleans Museum of Art

2. go to the Audubon Zoo
He has gone to the Audubon Zoo

3. take a river cruise on the Delta Queen
He has taken a river . . . .

4. take a boat tour of the swamps
He has taken a boat tour of . . .

5. become familiar with the French Quarter
He has become

6. eat in different restaurants
He has eaten

7. learn about jazz
He has learned

8. speak a lot of English
He has spoken

9. share a Thanksgiving turkey with some American families
He has

10. learn a lot about American culture

11. watch fireworks over the Mississippi River

12. attend some jazz concerts

13. see the place where Andrew Jackson fought the Battle of New Orleans

_____

14. make plans to visit all fifty states

_____

15. grow comfortable here

_____

Exercise C: Simple Past Tense vs. Present Perfect Tense

Please write the correct verb form (*simple past tense* or *present perfect tense*) in the sentences below. Use the simple past tense for actions that happened at a specific past time, such as *yesterday, last month, in 1999*. Use the present perfect tense for actions that started in the past and continue to the present, with time expressions such as *since 1999* or *for the past three years*.

1. Roberto and Bruno _____ in the United States for several years. (live)

2. Their family _____ in New Orleans in 1998. (arrive)

3. Bruno _____ many new and curious things since that time. (see)

4. Roberto _____ English for the past several years. (study)

5. They _____ to three concerts at Preservation Hall last year. (go)

6. Last Fourth of July, the Baroni family _____ the fireworks over the river. (watch)

7. Roberto and Bruno _____ a lot of English since they arrived. (learn)

8. Bruno and his friends _____ a famous battle site last month. (visit)

9. Roberto and Sylvia _____ at a marvelous restaurant last night. (eat)

10. The Baronis _____ a river cruise with some friends a month ago. (take)

Exercise D: Expressions of Comparison

Compare New York City and Rome, Italy. Use the following information to make your statements of comparison. Express your own point of view.

Example: New York—Rome (large)
New York is larger than Rome.

1. New York—Rome (dirtier)

   _____

2. New York—Rome (noisier)

   _____

3. New York—Rome (more modern)

   _____

4. New York—Rome (more interesting)

   _____

5. New York—Rome (more commercial)

   _____

6. New York—Rome (exciting)

   _____

7. New York—Rome (older)

   _____

8. New York—Rome (more beautiful)

   _____

9. New York—Rome (more historical)

   _____

10. New York—Rome (more familiar to Bruno)

   _____

Exercise E: Cohesion

The italicized part of each sentence below refers the reader to another point of information from Reading 10. Check Reading 10 for each point. Please circle the letter below the question to show the correct reference.

1. *We* came here from Italy by plane.
   Who does *we* refer to?

   a. Bruno

   b. the relatives

   c. Bruno and his family

2. Since *that time*, I have seen many curious and exciting places.
   What does *that time* refer to?

   a. coming to the United States by plane

   b. saying good-bye

   c. leaving Italy and coming to the United States

3. *It* was very different from Rome, my hometown.
   What does *it* refer to?

   a. New Orleans

   b. Italy

   c. the United States

4. While some areas of town seemed clean and modern, *others* appeared old and dirty.
   What does *others* refer to?

   a. other areas of Rome

   b. other areas of New Orleans

   c. other areas of the United States

5. *It* has been difficult because Italian is very different from English.
   What does *it* refer to?

   a. Italian grammar

   b. learning English

   c. idioms

6. Italian grammar seems *more regular* and *less idiomatic*.

   What is understood? *More regular* than what? *Less idiomatic* than what?

   a. than English grammar

   b. than American culture

   c. than the history of New Orleans

7. I speak English almost *like a native* now.

   What is understood? *Like a native* does what?

   a. speaks English

   b. speaks Italian

   c. uses Italian grammar

8. This is *our* new home.

   Who does *our* refer to?

   a. Mr. and Mrs. Baroni's

   b. Bruno and his family's

   c. Bruno and Roberto's

9. I *also* hope to visit Italy soon.

   What does *also* include?

   a. visiting all fifty states

   b. seeing my old friends

   c. visiting New Orleans

10. I don't want *them* to forget me.

    Who does *them* refer to?

    a. my parents

    b. all fifty states

    c. my grandparents and all my old friends

Exercise F: Cohesion (Connection)

Complete the following sentences. Please circle the letter below the sentence to choose the correct connecting word.

1. Bruno arrived in the United States on March 4, 1998. _____, he has seen and done a lot.

    a. Then

    b. Since then

    c. After that

2. _____, New Orleans was very strange to him. Now he feels comfortable in the city.

    a. At first

    b. Afterwards

    c. Finally

3. _____ some areas of New Orleans seemed clean and modern to Bruno, others seemed old and dirty.

    a. On the other hand

    b. Because

    c. While

4. In the beginning, New Orleans seemed small and uninteresting to Bruno. _____ it seems friendly and charming.

    a. Then

    b. Later

    c. Now

5. _____ Bruno first arrived, he felt so confused and lost.

    a. While

    b. When

    c. Where

6. English was difficult for Bruno to learn. _____, he speaks well now.

    a. Nevertheless

    b. At that point

    c. Because

7. Bruno has learned a lot of English. He has _____ learned a lot about American culture.

    a. if

    b. also

    c. but

8. Bruno has seen the place _____ Jackson fought the Battle of New Orleans.

    a. why

    b. when

    c. where

9. Bruno still has a lot to learn, _____ he feels comfortable here now.

    a. but

    b. and

    c. so

10. _____ Bruno wants to see more places in the United States, he is planning a trip across the country.

    a. After

    b. Before

    c. Because

Notes and Questions on the Organization of Reading 10

Part A: Paragraphs

Reading 10 tells the story of Bruno's stay in the United States. There are four paragraphs. Look back at those paragraphs. Identify the three basic parts within the system of paragraphs: *introduction, body,* and *conclusion.* Tell why you think so.

Part B: Order

The title of Reading 10 suggests a period of time. There is an important date in the introduction. You might, therefore, expect the order of information to be chronological. However, it is not. The following questions will help you decide what it is.

1. What does the writer say about the time since his arrival? How is it divided in the introduction? What are the subtopics?

2. Which subtopic does the writer discuss first? How does the writer get into that subtopic?

3. Which subtopic is next? How many examples does the writer give within that subtopic?

4. How does the writer conclude the discussion of the subtopics? Does the writer add new information?

Reading 10 uses *classification* as a tool to organize the information. The writer organizes the contents of time. *Contrasts* help to show change and progression within the period of time.

Take a moment to review all the different ways to order information. Next, go on to Model 10.

1. _____

2. _____

3. _____

4. _____

5. _____

6. _____

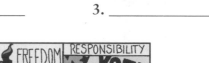

7. _____

Model 10 (Exposition)

Life in New Orleans

August 1, 1999, was an important day! On that day, I arrived in the United States. I traveled to New Orleans from Mexico by plane. I came with my cousin, Sylvia. We were so scared! We didn't know anyone in New Orleans and we had to find a place to live. Since that time, I have seen and done a lot. I have also learned many new things.

At first, I didn't like New Orleans. It was very different from Mexico City, my hometown. It seemed quieter and less interesting. I felt homesick for the excitement of Mexico City. Since then, I have become acquainted with New Orleans and I like it much better. I have discovered Tipitina's, Snug Harbor, and the Maple Leaf where local musicians play. I really like the music of the Neville Brothers. I don't have a lot of time for fun, but my boyfriend, Bruno, and I enjoy these places on the weekend. I have visited Lafayette and other Louisiana towns where people still speak French and keep their old ways. I love all the interesting accents. Now I think that New Orleans and the area around it are almost as exciting as Mexico City.

When I arrived, I already knew a lot of English, but I still needed some practice. Since then, I have become very fluent and my accent is much better. It hasn't been easy because English is a difficult language. It seems less regular and more idiomatic than Spanish. Nevertheless, I am proud of my English now. I have also learned a lot about American culture. Each person seems to have more freedom, but each person has more responsibility, too. I have never been so free and worked so hard! I have met many American students and talked to them. One American friend invites me to her house often. Last November, I celebrated Thanskgiving with her family. Sylvia went, too. I am beginning to feel at home in New Orleans now.

I plan to stay in New Orleans until I graduate from college. Then, I plan to go back to Mexico City. What about my boyfriend, Bruno? I don't know. We haven't really talked about the future. Now I am enjoying the present.

Caption Writing

Please write a sentence under each picture on page 132 or in your notebook.

Composition 10

Instructions for Student's Composition

1. On 8¹/2 x 11 inch loose-leaf notebook paper, write a composition about your stay in the United States or your life in the city where you live. Divide your composition into two parts: what you have seen/done and what you have learned. Give your composition a title.

2. Write four paragraphs. Remember to indent and leave margins. Put the following information in your paragraphs:

   PARAGRAPH 1. Where do you live? How long have you lived there? Show that you are dividing the topic into two parts: *seen/done* and *learned*.

   PARAGRAPH 2. Describe the beginning. What was different between the old place and the new place? What have you seen/done in the new place?

   PARAGRAPH 3. What have you learned in the new place?

   PARAGRAPH 4. Conclude with your future plans.

3. Take what you need from Model 10. Let it help you with grammar, vocabulary, ideas, and organization.

4. Your composition should look like this:

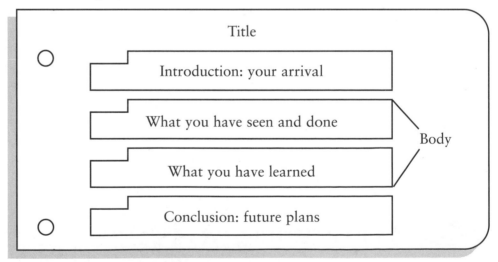

 # Connecting

Use a search engine (such as Netscape, Yahoo, or Excite). Choose a holiday that is celebrated in the United States, such as Thanksgiving, Fourth of July, Halloween, Presidents' Day, or Memorial Day. Can you find out when it is celebrated, how people celebrate it, and why it is celebrated? Tell a partner about the holiday.

Appendix

Irregular Verb Forms

Present	Simple Past Tense Form	Past Participle
be	was/were	been
become	became	become
break	broke	broken
build	built	built
catch	caught	caught
come	came	come
do	did	done
drive	drove	driven
eat	ate	eaten
fall	fell	fallen
feel	felt	felt
find	found	found
forget	forgot	forgotten
get	got	gotten
give	gave	given
go	went	gone
grow	grew	grown
have	had	had
hit	hit	hit
hurt	hurt	hurt
know	knew	known
leave	left	left
make	made	made
meet	met	met
ride	rode	ridden
ring	rang	rung
rise	rose	risen
run	ran	run
say	said	said
see	saw	seen
send	sent	sent
sit	sat	sat
speak	spoke	spoken
swim	swam	swum
take	took	taken
teach	taught	taught
tell	told	told
think	thought	thought
throw	threw	thrown
wear	wore	worn
write	wrote	written

Vocabulary List

(The numbers refer to units where words first appear.)

accent (3)

accident (7)

acquainted (10)

advertisement (6)

alarm clock (1)

algebra (1)

alive (10)

all in all (1)

ancient (10)

angry (5)

apartment (1)

apologize (5)

appear (10)

area (10)

artistic (9)

attractive (9)

average (2)

bath (5)

bayou (10)

be crazy about (2)

beach (7)

become (4)

bedroom (1)

beg (7)

believe (9)

bell (4)

bilingual (6)

block (4)

board (7)

boss (5)

break down (5)

bring (4)

brr (8)

build (2)

business institute (6)

careful (4)

carry (3)

catch (a flight or plane) (7)

cemetery (4)

certainly (2)

change (6)

charming (10)

chemistry (1)

coach (2)

coat (3)

cold (8)

comfortable (9)

complete (6)

computer program (6)

confused (10)

contact (6)

cool (8)

corner (4)

corporation (6)

cousin (7)

crazy (2)

crowded (3)

cruise (10)

culture (10)

curious (10)

curly (9)

dangerous (4)

dark (2)

date (9)

deadline (5)

decide (7)

defeat (10)

definite (2)

definitely (8)

delicious (3)

department store (3)

deserve (5)

diet (9)

difficult (5)

diploma (6)

directions (4)

dirty (10)

discouraged (1)

dishes (1)

down (3)

downtown (5)

dress up (2)

dry (3)

early (3)

easy (4)

employee (5)

especially (9)

excellent (6)

exciting (10)

executive assistant (6)

exercise (1)

exhausted (5)

fairly (2)

fall (8)

familiar (10)

fat (2)

fault (7)

finally (5)

fireworks (10)

fix (5)

flat (7)

flight (7)

follow (4)

forget (3)

form (5)

fortunately (7)

Fourth of July (10)

free time (3)

friendly (2)

frustrating (5)

funny (3)

future plans (2)

get off (5)

glad (5)

grand (10)

green (2)

guess (7)

guest (4)

hat (3)

heavy (8)

history (10)

homesick (3)

hometown (10)

hot (5)

humid (8)

hurry (3)

hurt (7)

idiomatic (10)

ill (2)

important (5)

improve (2)

in a hurry (3)

in a row (1)

inconvenience (7)

inexpensive (4)

intend (10)

intersection (4)

interview (6)

IRS (Internal Revenue
Service) (5)

jeans (2)

kitchen table (1)

language (6)

late (5)

later (5)

laugh (3)

lead (4)

left (4)

location (4)

long (1)

look (2)

lost (10)

loud (9)

magazine (1)

marry (2)

marvelous (10)

melt (8)

mile (4)

miss (3)

modern (10)

monument (10)

mood (8)

more (4)

narrow (2)

native (10)

nervous (5)

news (1)

old (2)

outgoing (2)

parking lot (4)

part time (1)

passenger (5)

pecan pie (3)

personality (2)

physical education (2)

pick up (9)

pleasant (2)

point (4)

position (6)

puddle (3)

put away (9)

quiet (9)

radio (1)

rain (3)

reference (6)

regards (3)

regular (10)

relative (10)

relieved (7)

repair shop (7)

request (6)

reservation (7)

reserved (9)

responsible (6)

resumé (6)

right (4)

ring (4)

roommate (9)

science (2)

season (8)

send (3)

sensitive (2)

serious (9)

shave (1)

shine (8)

shorthand (6)

shower (1)

sidewalk (3)

site (10)

skill (6)

small (1)

smile (2)

smooth (7)

snow (8)

snowball (8)

snowman (8)

social (9)

splendid (10)

spreadsheets (6)

spring (8)

stay in shape (1)

stop (4)

straight (1)

strange (10)

stuck (8)

summer (8)

surprising (9)

swamp (10)

tall (2)

taste (3)

temperature (8)

terrible (5)

terrific (10)

Thanksgiving (10)

thin (2)

think (5)

tidy (9)

tire (7)

tiring (1)

together (1)

tourist commission (6)

traffic light (4)

true (2)

try on (3)

T-shirt (2)

turkey (10)

turn (4)

turn down (9)

turn off (9)

turn on (9)

turn up (9)

type (6)

typical (5)

umbrella (3)

understanding (5)

unexciting (10)

unfortunately (7)

unique (10)

unpleasant (8)

up (3)

upset (3)

usually (1)

valuable (5)

veer (4)

wait (5)

wake (1)

warm (3)

way (5)

weather (8)

well-organized (9)

wide (10)

winter (8)

wonderful (3)

word processing (6)

work experience (6)

worry (2)

Skills Index

LANGUAGE (Grammar, Usage, and Mechanics)

READING

SPEAKING, LISTENING, AND VIEWING

TECHNOLOGY

WRITING

VOCABULARY

Adjectives 4, 16, 28, 42, 54, 66, 80, 94, 108, 122
Adverbs 4, 16, 28, 42, 54, 80, 94, 108
Antonyms 16, 109
Expressions 4, 16, 28, 94, 95
Frequency words 6–7
Nouns 4, 16, 28, 42, 54, 66, 80, 94, 108, 122
Recognizing 54, 68, 123
Verbs 4, 16, 28, 42, 54, 66, 80, 94, 95, 108, 122
Vocabulary list 136–138
Weather-related 95, 96